Hebrew Literature
in the Wake
of the Holocaust

The ongoing program of the International Center for University Teaching of Jewish Civilization is sponsored by the Joint Program for Jewish Education of the State of Israel—Ministry of Education and Culture, The Jewish Agency for Israel, and The World Zionist Organization.

Thanks are expressed to the Ashdown Trust for its support of this publication, through the good offices of Mr. Clive Marks.

Hebrew Literature
in the Wake
of the Holocaust

Edited by
Leon I. Yudkin

Published in Conjunction with the International Center
for University Teaching of Jewish Civilization

Rutherford ● Madison ● Teaneck
Fairleigh Dickinson University Press
London and Toronto: Associated University Presses

Associated University Presses
440 Forsgate Drive
Cranbury, NJ 08512

Associated University Presses
25 Sicilian Avenue
London WC1A 2QH, England

Associated University Presses
P.O. Box 338, Port Credit
Mississauga, Ontario
Canada L5G 4L8

The paper used in this publication meets the requirements
of the American National Standard for Permanence of Paper
for Printed Library Materials Z39.48-1984.

Library of Congress Cataloging-in-Publication Data

Hebrew literature in the wake of the Holocaust / edited by Leon
I. Yudkin.
　　p.　cm.
Published in conjunction with the International Center for
University Teaching of Jewish Civilization.
Includes bibliographical references.
ISBN 0-8386-3499-0 (alk. paper)
　　1. Israeli literature—History and criticism.　2. Holocaust,
Jewish (1939–1945), in literature.　3. Holocaust survivors in
University Teaching of Jewish Civilization.
PJ5012.H65H43　1993
892.4′09358—dc20　　　　　　　　　　　　　　　　92-54455
　　　　　　　　　　　　　　　　　　　　　　　　　　　CIP

PRINTED IN THE UNITED STATES OF AMERICA

Dedicated to
SIDNEY MUSHER
in recognition of his passionate devotion
to Jewish Peoplehood

Contents

Introduction

LEON I. YUDKIN

To talk about the literature of the Holocaust might seem to be a contradiction in terms. Is not literature an expression of delight, an attempt to seize its subject and turn it into art? And is not the Holocaust the ultimate horror, life's utter negation? How, then, can literature look there for its content? And how can there be an esthetic of such material?

And yet the question can be turned on its head. The Holocaust has happened and, with its foreshadowings and reverberations, constitutes one of the influential occurrences of the century. Perhaps, indeed, it is the major event in its moral implications, for what it tells us about man's actual and potential behavior. The scale too is enormous, the events worldwide, some of the survivors still alive, the horror everywhere. How can it *not* be written about, unless literature is to be trivialized and confined to the periphery?

The Holocaust was perpetrated in many places and over many years, and its implications are human and universal. Yet, it was specifically directed against certain peoples and, more than any others, against the Jews. The war against the Jews was conducted with a large measure of success—in Nazi terms—killing over a third of the world's Jewish population, and almost obliterating the European component of that people. This is not an observation in mitigation of the general significance of the event, only a note of its accompanying specificity. The Holocaust is both universal and Jewish.

Literature has to take account of what has happened—what has happened in recent history, what has happened to people—because that is the subject of literature. The investigation of the literary treatment of the Holocaust has been particularly nurtured over recent years, and it is by no means coming to an end. Such analysis is to be welcomed, both as a contribution toward the understanding of the event and toward the understanding of the writing. What do literary genres mean in this context? Is the generic division of the same order as with other literature? What does the investigation of such literature tell us about literature in general? Is the Holocaust an event *sui generis,* and must the literature then be of that order? Who are the legitimate bearers of such material, and how is it properly conveyed? These questions arise again and again, in the present volume too.

That the Holocaust has particular significance for Hebrew literature is clear. Hebrew writing is quintessentially Jewish, and so must absorb the impact of the fury directed against itself. But it is more than that. It is also the antithesis of that event, the assertion of survival. We might expect Hebrew literature of the Holocaust to develop its own color and character, while still sharing the general perspectives of Holocaust literature overall.

This volume is devoted to the investigation of Holocaust literature in Hebrew, written in Israel. The theme was considered in a workshop organized by the International Center for University Teaching of Jewish Civilization, held in Jerusalem with participants from Israel and from many countries where Holocaust literature is taught within a variety of academic disciplines. The contributors to the book are writers, critics and teachers. Some are witnesses, some children of survivors, some more distant observers; but all are concerned with the subject. In the wake of those momentous, dreadful events, we confront their representation through the various means available in words. Some of the effort of this representation is described here.

Hebrew Literature
in the Wake
of the Holocaust

Narrative Perspectives in Holocaust Literature

LEON I. YUDKIN

Holocaust literature, for our purposes, is writing that takes its subject and starting point from the war conducted against the Jews in Europe from 1933 to 1945. Although that is the point of origin, the continuation is less certain, less defined, and less crystallized. The effects go on, and writing allows these to move in different directions. The writer as narrator may be the prime focus of the narrative or a reporter of a distant event. Such an account may be a chronicle in which the chronicler is the principal actor or a subsidiary actor. Or, he may not be involved in the story at all. He may be the unwitting carrier of the substantive narrative, the unwilling discoverer, or the invisible and inconspicuous presenter—in which case, we would like to find out where the narrative focus lies.

In this attempt to present some narrative perspectives evident in Holocaust literature, no perspective will be excluded; all will be admitted, and there will be no conferral of legitimacy on any particular literary genre. We will not argue that the writing of nonsurvivors or nonwitnesses is less authentic than that of primary accounts by witnesses, survivors, and others who bear the historical experience on their own flesh. We will also accept the text as a literary datum on its own terms, and it is the text that will decide whether it is diary, memoir, biography, story, fable, drama, essay, or history. What interests us is the variety of literary types dealing with the subject, and the manner in which the narrative perspective takes its position from the event described.

Characteristic of the Holocaust is death—violent, mass-produced, anonymous. This death is not necessarily meaningless, since it is life which is meaningful, and death is usually random, mistimed, arbitrary, unjust, and painful. But the additional ingredient is the Jewish component, for the Holocaust intended (and nearly achieved) the extermination of an entire people. The survivor, and indeed anyone writing with an awareness of the event, has to incorporate the sense of demonic hatred, violently expressed in action and specifically directed against the Jew.

Inevitably, this will give rise to a question and an inference. The question is why this should be so. Does it stem from "election"? Or, does the historical experience signal a disgrace? The consequential inference involves the next stage—what is to be done. Holocaust literature carries a reflective consciousness, which produces causes, consequences, and lessons. These are complicated by the impingement of national or individual considerations, and are morally muddied by the possibly ambivalent inferences drawn.

Doubt has been expressed as to whether there can be an appropriate literature of the Holocaust. "A novel about Auschwitz is not a novel, or else it is not about Auschwitz," wrote Elie Wiesel.[1] Adorno's famous pronouncement about not writing poetry after Auschwitz also formulates the disjunction.[2] And yet, there are novels (long works of fiction), stories, plays, poems, as well as diaries, memoirs, and speculations, which engage the subject. The theme may impose inordinate strains, but it is precisely the attempt to absorb the shock into the literary fabric that creates the work.

In terms of literary history, this is not a new difficulty. Some generations ago, Expressionist literature broke down traditional literary modes—meter and rhyme in poetry, coherence of structure, consecutive language, the concept of character—in order to represent the violence and breakdown of its subject, namely, the world. However, the genres were bent and not broken. They have resurrected themselves, and they are back where they were. A novel is still a novel, even if on the border of memoir, even if it reverses traditional expectations. Adorno might have charged Celan with incongruous lyricism in "Todesfuge," but the alternative is to write another sort of poem. It is for the reader to judge the degree of discordance between the framework and the material.

In the meantime, we will accept Holocaust literature for what it is, for what it deals with. The intent of this literature, shaped by the subject, may transcend normal historical concerns,[3] but the forms are remarkably resilient. A bottle may hold water or acid, but it remains a container for liquid, with a convenient point of access. Through the violence of twentieth-century history and through the assault on humanity, literary forms have stayed in their place from the previous century. No equivalent to the invention of the novel has yet appeared, although many directions have been changed and original intentions subverted. Rosenfeld and Langer,[4] among others, have demonstrated that the thrust of earlier literary models has been reversed; whereas in the *Bildungsroman,* for example, a course of progress is charted, in the Holocaust narrative the movement goes from life into death. The normal expectations generated by life itself are stood on their head. But even these reversals are executed within the traditional shapes and structures. Indeed, it is the very adherence to what is possible and familiar that makes the content all the more startling, bleak and even, as the echoes ring out repeatedly, unbelievable. We are reading poems, stories, apparently normal accounts of what would otherwise be inexpressible.

An initial and primary difficulty inherent in dealing with Holocaust literature is the determination of its scope. Is such writing solely the documentation of the atrocity, the process of the Final Solution? Or can it also be related to what was on the periphery during the critical years? Beyond this, is the category only applicable to the years 1933–45, or is it carried beyond that date? If so, is it a weight pressing on the individual or the group, on the survivor, the survivor's kin or, indeed, on all of us? Are we talking about a specific concatenation of events, or about a recurrent human condition? Is there a foreshadowing in antecedent work that should be included under this heading? And, if the category is so comprehensive, is it meaningful at all?

While these and other theoretical questions may be raised, for our purposes it is clear that "Holocaust literature" is a legitimate and self-validating concept, whatever the dates, referents, determinants, or authors. This may reflect directly on the subject or obliquely bear its consciousness. Clearly, too, we cannot rule any author out of consideration on the basis of religion, affiliation, race, nationality, or viewpoint. Rosenfeld's "net" is comprehensive for the years following 1945, although the category is required to relate to the event and to Jews: ". . . all novels about Jewish suffering written in the post-Holocaust period must implicate the Holocaust, whether it is expressly named or not."[5] Without intending in any way to reduce the Jewish specificity of the event, I would like to accept this perspective and enlarge it to include any suffering—Jewish and non-Jewish—that arises from the experience. Thus, what we are treating is what derives from the Holocaust or, more speculatively, foreshadows it. Sometimes, the link is explicit or manifest; on other occasions, it may be secondary or oblique.

This indirect sense of Holocaust literature is, undoubtedly, difficult to define. It transcends Nietzsche's death of God, although it also incorporates it. Similarly, it goes beyond the expressionist effort to match the breakdown of civilization with the breaking up of language patterns, meters, rhythms, structures, and coherences. It enters and attempts to incorporate the experience of death as its own object. In Holocaust literature, death is not part of life, but the totality of being become subject.

Documentary Re-Creation

The great range of narrative possibilities within the scope of a subject so determined and dark, becomes apparent on examination. In this study we are dealing not with the narrative content itself, but only with the placement of the narrative voice. Genre clearly shapes a good deal of this, as does the imitation of a genre, or the fictional adoption of a particular posture. Moral and historical responsibility must press hard on the author of Holocaust literature who, within these awesome confines, is not only telling a story but also conveying the sense of an event. The survivor is witness to what has been lived through, and there are survivor-authors who see it as their function to bear reliable testimony. However, as events do not exist only in themselves but in a symbiotic relationship with the observer, this testimony is multilayered. The witness sees only part, and what is seen is shaded by subjectivity.

Genre determines the shape of the narrative. There are diaries (testimonies) that look like novels, and novels that look like diaries. Ka-Tzetnik's *House of Dolls*[6] is an example of the former. This is a novel very close to the author's experience of incarceration in Auschwitz. The principal narrative focus is Daniella. The content is informative about the Cracow ghetto and about Auschwitz itself, although the form is fictional. It has a traditional shape, is divided into chapters, and moves the action forward in a chronological manner. But it also backtracks through flashbacks and memories, and is dotted with dreams, nightmares, and fantasies. The story opens with a school trip, the first of Daniella's life, and from that point proceeds to consistently more negative events. The structure then is novelistic, although it reverses the novel's traditional movement by sending the heroine into the abyss.

Although *House of Dolls* has a novel's structure, its furniture is of the actual world. It is required to adhere to historical truth, to the facts of the war, the camps, the cruelty and annihilation. In this way, it differs from a more recent tendency (as expressed, for example, in *Sophie's Choice*) to mix actuality and fantasy in such a way as to distort the event, and even to convey a picture quite other than the one obtained by straightforward observation and absorption of facts. The narrative voice is not neutral. It comments omnisciently on the thoughts and feelings of the characters, on attitudes of individuals, groups, and nations, on the past in contrast to the present. It also speculates on the motivation and lifestyle of the torturers outside of "working hours." This is the representative commentator, wondering how such a thing is possible, after describing it in detail.

If *House of Dolls* is a documentary account dressed up as a novel, Marguerite Duras's *La Douleur*[7] is a novel in the form of a diary. Set in Paris towards the end of the war, the point of view is that of a woman awaiting the release of her beloved, Robert, from a German concentration camp. Although she is assured of his return, she indulges in romantic fantasies of his death, of him "having spoken [her] name just before dying."[8] Although this seems to be a diary in genre, there are giveaway signs that it cannot be such in the literal sense. There is projection, a diary entry written with hindsight, as for example in the aside about one who was to die later that night (p. 29). The fiction is of a diary discovered forty years after its composition. The form lends urgency and credibility, conveying the sense of the time and place. The work is of a woman riven by emotional forces, yearning for her absent lover and hating the Germans. We also observe the sensitivities of a Frenchwoman commenting ironically that De Gaulle mourns Roosevelt's death, but is silent about the deportees (p. 42). The diary form allows the exploration of the subject as the immediate experience of extreme events. Consider the circumstances—the unprecedentedly violent war, the torture of the beloved, the victory. And then the return home. What better way to explore the changing faces of hope, despair, love, vengeance, and reconciliation? Duras's narrator also searches her own consciousness for signs of identity problems, and even questions who she herself is. Her self-identification with the object of her love is total: "Like him I have not eaten for 17 days. Like him I have not slept for 17 days" (p. 74). But Robert is paralyzed by his experience. He cannot speak of it, answer questions, write or read about it. The author tries to communicate the experience of the accumulated, growing knowledge of the horror; the truth is gradually being discovered. Her reconciliation comes with the acceptance of the fact that the agent, Rabier, is not really a person, but just a stand-in for the German police (p. 120). So she defends him at a later trial.

We can see that quasi-reportage of the event can assume various forms, even some which may belie their normal nature. The objective is to capture the reality. A diary situates the writer in the place and time of its subject (although Duras's narrator is just outside the event). The novel (Ka-Tzetnik's is a third-person account) places its characters right in the cauldron, but adopts a fictional form that is more distancing than is a journal. Both constitute an interesting interplay between genre and point of view.

Reconstruction of Event

Apart from genre, it is the two poles of narrative focus and narrative position that situate the work. All fictions are to some degree reconstructions. But there is a difference between the attempt to recapture a situation personally experienced, and the creation of an imagined account. Both *Sophie's Choice*[9] and *The White Hotel*[10] place the Holocaust within sprawling fictions, incidents recalled by or happening to the fictional characters. In both cases, the narrative victims of the violent excesses of the Nazis are non-Jews. Thomas's novel is a tapestry of effects, and the account of the Babi Yar massacre is taken from Anatoli Kuznetsov's novel of that name.[11] The scene is so shocking that Lisa, the narrative focus, half imagines that it is not really happening at all: "There are things so far beyond belief that it ought to be possible to awake from them" (p. 215). Frau Elisabeth Erdman, a Catholic, originally of Kiev but later living in Vienna, shifts in her imagination from one scene to another (a move finally confirmed by the novel's dream conclusion). Her identity is subjectively doubtful. She says that she is "probably half-Jewish" (p. 154),[12] the word "probably" conveying an unconscious rejection of her father, and so, too, of the disgrace and contempt associated with Jewishness (p. 168). But the fantasy of the "Camp" (section 6), invoked at the point of the horrifying slaughter at the ravine, is of a Promised Land, an Israel in which she is to be resurrected and welcomed. There, she would also welcome others. *The White Hotel* is not a Holocaust novel. It is a novel in which twentieth-century violence plays a part through the experiences of a rootless, searching, ethnically and religiously ambiguous woman.

Sophie's Choice also sets the Holocaust within the framework of a novel primarily located elsewhere. Here, the narrative starting point is Brooklyn, and the narrator, an aspiring writer from Virginia who arrives in New York in 1947. The novel reverses the normal expectations of the Holocaust in literature. As refracted by Stingo, the narrator, it is the Pole, the lovely Sophie, who is the victim, tortured by the Jew, the mentally deranged Nathan. They have an apartment in the Brooklyn house where Stingo lives, and the narrator becomes privy to their ongoing story as well as to their past. Sophie is a Pole, but a survivor. Nathan is a Jew, born in America, privileged and brilliant, but unstable. Presumably, the book's thrust is to challenge stereotypes. We know, after all, that there were non-Jewish victims in Europe, just as we know that many Jews flourish in America. So why not universalize the events? Just as *The White Hotel* uses other documentary accounts in the Babi Yar section, so the Auschwitz section here is peppered with documentary allusions and historical references. Rudolf Hoess, the commandant of Auschwitz, is a major character in the novel; he is presented quite sympathetically, based on his own testimony.

Sophie's Choice is not just fiction. Styron has written an introduction to Richard Rubenstein's *The Cunning of History*,[13] and that work is invoked approvingly in the novel (p. 315). What primarily interests Styron about Rubenstein's work, and indeed about

Auschwitz itself, is one of its "dual functions" as "a vast enclave dedicated to the practice of slavery" (the other function, of course, is murder). Rubenstein labels Auschwitz "a society of total domination," and this concept, marking a further point in the continuum of the history of slavery, clearly fits Styron's own interests as a historian of the subject.[14] But slavery, however inhuman and cruel, is utilitarian and has an economic base. To see Auschwitz in either of its "functions" within this spectrum, constitutes a monstrous distortion of its nature. Although work was carried out at Auschwitz in the Buna factory, production was not only secondary but nonexistent. Primo Levi writes: "As will be told, the Buna factory, on which the Germans were busy for four years and for which countless of us suffered and died, never produced a pound of synthetic rubber."[15] If we observe the evident facts, we must draw the conclusion that Auschwitz was not interested in slavery, much less in production. It was set up to kill the Jews, and many others as well. It is this other function that it fulfilled so efficiently. Places other than Auschwitz did make use of the prisoners for labor— industrial works such as Krupps, for example. Within the camp, however, labor was a facade, and a barely convincing one at that.[16] As for the theory of "domination" as an end in itself, that also wears rather thin. What sort of domination is exercised over corpses? That is what almost all of the inmates became, and the remainder certainly would have become had not the liberation intervened. The attempts of the author to apply a rational framework and universalizing typology to the events of the Third Reich do not square with the known facts. This would not necessarily matter in a work of fiction, were it not for its tendentiousness. *Sophie's Choice* is not just an entertainment, but a didactic opus. One element that the author clearly finds uncomfortable in an understanding of the Holocaust is its Jewish specificity. It is an element that is not easily accommodated by a historian of world slavery.

Reflection on the Survivor

The traumatic experience lives on for decades after the traumatic events themselves. Recent Holocaust literature from America is also the literature of survivors. This last sentence has been phrased in a deliberately ambiguous manner. The "of" can mean "written by" and it can also mean "relating to." Holocaust literature is no less legitimate for not being written by those directly affected. The Jewish writer will necessarily incorporate important recent Jewish history, which has to make an ongoing impact. The American Jewish writer may have a distant but still very engaged view. Both Isaac Bashevis Singer and Saul Bellow were in the United States at the time of the Holocaust. Bashevis Singer had emigrated from Poland in 1934, and Bellow is Canadian-born. But both (contrary to some strange impression) have written fiction with the Holocaust as its subject. Both portray heroes who have not only gone through the dreadful experience, but who, decades later, continue to live that experience every day of their lives.

Herman Broder, the central figure of *Enemies*,[17] lives a weird, secretive, hand-to-mouth existence in the Brooklyn of the 1960s. He is a survivor who was saved in Poland by hiding in a hayloft for three years. Having assumed that his wife Tamara had been shot and killed, he has rewarded Yadwiga, the servant who helped him, by marrying her. He is also carrying on an affair with Masha, another survivor. He then discovers that his first wife, Tamara, has been saved after all. Now, as a man involved with three women, each of whom assumes that she is his exclusive, or at least primary, object of affection, it is not surprising that Herman is living in a sort of bunker, covering up his tracks from public scrutiny as far as possible. The point is that he is continuing to live his old life in the present, in his consciousness (he is constantly oppressed by fear of Nazis), in his personal involvements, and in his work. He is not committed to America in any authentic way. His work is to write speeches and essays for a Rabbi Lampert, wheeler-dealer on a massive scale. But he will not be pinned down, not by the rabbi who wants to help him, nor by any of the three women who seek to involve him, and not by the general public, demanding to establish his whereabouts.

What then is Herman Broder? His situation derives from the experience of being a hunted Jew, a witness to wholesale death. He has survived but, as he says, "Anyone who's gone through all that I have is no longer a part of the world" (p. 25). The most pervasive sense in the novel is of death-in-life. Tamara says almost the same thing as Herman, in almost identical words: "I really no longer think of myself as being part of this world" (p. 82). She has miraculously survived after being shot, but one bullet is still lodged inside her. That bullet symbolizes the presence of death in an apparently vital organism. Herman is a survivor, but so are the three women. The narrative effect is one of ambiguity. The margins are blurred. Death is in life, but life is in death, with the possibility of revival. Herman reflects on Tamara: "Whenever he was with her, he experienced the miracle of resurrection" (p. 106). He seems to be present everywhere, but he also keeps disappearing, conclusively at the novel's end. And who are the "enemies"? One might assume the Nazis. But Herman refers to Masha as his enemy (p. 201), and Masha, after herself shouting out "Enemies" (p. 209), kills herself. We want to know about possible resolutions and, indeed, in the epilogue, Yadwiga has Herman's baby, and Tamara helps out. But Herman has vanished, still retaining his old habits. The narrator speculates that he has ". . . killed himself or was hiding somewhere in an American version of his Polish hayloft" (p. 220).

Bellow's Sammler[18] is also a survivor from Poland now living in America, and he also brings to the New World in the sixties the consciousness of what he has gone through. Although an intellectual, he is aware that "life is sacred" (p. 17). It is only intellectuals who do not understand what is basic, he avers, and who can talk about the "banality of evil" without seeing that the banality is only camouflage. Sammler's likeness to Broder lies in what he learns from that other experience, and applies in the here-and-now: "Like many people who had seen the world collapse once, Mr. Sammler entertained the possibility it might collapse twice" (p. 29). Sammler is also a symbol—of another generation, of another place, time, and life. He had also survived by being hidden during the war, in a mausoleum. He knows that he is now a symbol, but what is he to make of that? "He, personally, was a symbol. His friends and family had made him a judge and a priest. And of what was he a symbol? He didn't even know. Was it because he had survived? He hadn't even done that, since so much of the earlier person had disappeared. It wasn't surviving, it was only lasting" (p. 75). Broder and Sammler are both presences of death in the United States. They both take their bearings from that other existence, and now only live the life of a planet that receives light from the sun of a previous life. That earlier existence acts as a commentary on current possibilities and hopeful illusions, including those illusions fostered by H. G. Wells, in which Sammler had once indulged.

There is another such survivor figure invoked by Bellow in a later fiction, *The Bellarosa Connection*.[19] The question raised by the narrator is whether Fonstein is American or European. And the answer: "Fonstein for all his Jermyn Street boots and Italianate suits was still the man who had buried his mother in Venice and waited in his cell for Ciano to rescue him. . . . I believe that he was thinking intensively about his European origin and his American transformation: Part 1 and Part 2" (p. 21). Of course, the question raised about Europe and America transcends the geographical referent. It is about the nature of the person, and whether he is finally determined by his past or not. In this case, he is. But here, too, that split finds its echo in the narrator. He, too, is split between the genteel Philadelphia, where he has "made it" and New Jersey, whence he hails. There is a tension within himself, half-Jewish, half "Wasp," that is only resolved by finding a way into the past. The institute that he has founded and which he manages with such commercial success stands for that way into the past. It is an institute for remembering, the Mnemosyne Institute. He himself can never forget anything, however insignificant, and so he becomes that other kind of witness, a witness of record.

Narrative as Record

No genre blurs the line between documentary record and fiction more than those novels of the Holocaust which exalt perfect memory and exhort the narrator, as a sacred duty, to preserve the integrity of the event. Here, too, the line between narrator and narrated is blurred. In the novels/memoirs of Wiesel and Levi, the survivor is the narrator, telling of himself and of his own experience.

This is not to say that the narrators do not try to filter their experiences, invest them with meaning and form, and make them works of art. The art here also includes perspectives, angles, points of view that offer sense, morals, and lessons. Both Wiesel's and Levi's accounts are ethical to the highest degree, attempting to transmit but also to send back, to learn the lesson and to teach it, while conveying the events in all their horror.

Night is Wiesel's first work[20] and, in the words of one critic, the "foundation of the author's entire oeuvre."[21] He recounts his early tutelage at the feet of Moche the beadle, the mystic who had become witness. Once he had spoken of God and the way to Him, but now he only spoke of the slaughter of the Jews. The Hungarians of Sighet were only deported in 1944, after it seemed that Germany's defeat was assured. Indeed, that the deportations from Italy and Hungary came so late accounts for the existence of these major testimonies. Moche the beadle saw it as his exclusive obligation to bear witness, and this is the message of *Night*. No prophecy is required, just the conveying of accurate information. But, of course, this information is ignored. Even with the Germans actually in occupation of Sighet and a "Fascist" government installed, the Jews still believed that all would turn out well. The messenger of literal truth is rejected. This novel comes after the event, in place of the warning. It now informs the ignorant, innocent reader that what transpired was indeed unimaginable (except that it was acted out), the ultimate evil surpassing all that had gone before.

The witness in *Night* is a fourteen-year-old, although the material was written down over a decade later, when the author was already a young man. The youth enters the place "Auschwitz—no-one had ever heard that name" (p. 67). The camp inmates even greet his arrival with relief, so unaware are they of the terrible reality. The narrator is both on the scene and beyond it, identifying himself both as the adolescent in the camp and as the adult who knows what is to transpire. But *Night* is also a story of enlightenment, the acquisition of a truth which brings about a loss of faith and the death of God in the youth's pious heart. The move from Auschwitz (which had to be evacuated, in the face of the oncoming Russian army) to Buchenwald—including the episode of his father's death, followed by the youth's loss of interest in everything, until liberation by Jewish partisans at the end of the war—is recounted briefly and bleakly.

Primo Levi's account of incarceration at Auschwitz[22] in many ways parallels Wiesel's. Carefully contrived to highlight the significant, the narrator/author greatly prizes absolute accuracy. He was captured by the Fascist militia in Italy at the end of 1943, and was sent to Auschwitz in February 1944. In his case, as with Wiesel, the late date of his arrival accounts for his survival, although, as he indicates, only 8 out of the 125 sent there with him actually did survive. The structure of the work is original. As Levi explains in the preface: "The chapters have been written, not in logical succession, but in order of urgency." And their composition has a cathartic function, to achieve "an interior liberation."

Levi's *If This is a Man* is a work of reflection as well as narrative. The denouement is inevitable and known by the reader *ab initio*, although the descent into Auschwitz and the furniture of that hell are described more coolly and objectively than in other works. The reflective part considers not only the German apparatus of total domination, but also the transvaluation of values required on the part of the inmates to adjust and even, just possibly, to survive. There are two categories of people, "the drowned and the saved,"[23] a division of humanity to which the author frequently returns. Levi's training in chemistry, his need to understand, categorize, and analyze, led him to consider human types in terms of "The Periodic Table."[24] Thus, he can divide humanity on the basis of ancestors and descendants, gentiles and Jews: "I am the impurity that makes the zinc react. I am the grain of salt, of mustard" (p. 35). Chemistry, through the periodic table, represents the principle of order in the universe. Unfortunately, perhaps, the universe is too ordered. The oppressor will always remain the oppressor, and the victim always the victim.[25]

A Life Once Lived

The past has not disappeared. It continues to live on in memory, in current models, and as an echo of the ongoing torrent. In another sense though, the past can stand still. Some literary works attempt to frame this past, so that it looks quite separate. Alternatively, the past can visit the present, but appears congealed, unaffected by the currents of time and place that are always changing and undergoing revision.

Giorgio Bassani's *The Garden of the Finzi-Continis*[26] presents a picture of the life lived by a Jewish family in Ferrara before 1938 (the year of the introduction of racial laws into Italy), filtered through the recall of Micol, who says, "the memory of things is much more important than the possession of them" (p. 224). The events are recalled by the narrator from the perspective of 1957, more than a decade after the deportation and extermination. Only one of the Finzi-Continis managed to be buried in the family tomb. The others had been taken to Auschwitz. The novel is an idyll, as it tries to set a perfect scene of "magical suspense" (p. 86). But this is also an ambiguous scene. The narrator had been in love with Micol, but she had regarded him as a brother. What interested her was that he shared her way of looking at things, and that their common code encapsulated them in a single family, thus also precluding the possibility of erotic attraction. In her view, their shared vice consisted of "looking backwards as we went ahead" (p. 225). This is an idyll, because it creates a sense of distance. In this case, the distance in time is not very great, but it still exists, and thus that whole life becomes a hazy entity suitable for inspection from a distance.

Aharon Appelfeld's work is quite different, and it works differently. His tales are either set before the events of the war or during their aftermath, but not during the war itself. What links these two time zones is an imperviousness to the reality of the world around, as in *Badenheim 1939*,[27] where the Jewish society in the eponymous Austrian spa swims fretfully and unknowingly to its doom. The stories set beyond the catastrophe are of figures catatonically affected and unable to respond to the present.[28]

Both Bassani and Appelfeld have set up models of the past in their fiction, one positive and romantic, the other negative and deluded, and engage them in present time. For Bassani's narrator a dreamy haze envelops the narrative; Appelfeld's figure is governed by a pathological paralysis.

Dramatic Use of History

The events of the Holocaust provide a rich mine of moral dilemmas and problems. At no other point in history have so many people had to respond to such a total evil within a context of overwhelming power. How did the individuals respond, and how indeed could they have responded otherwise? No literary genre is more suited than drama to display the range and variety of response and to subject it to dialectical investigation.

Rolf Hochhuth's play *The Representative*[29] is written in indignation at the way in which Vatican leaders reacted to Nazism, but it is also supported by a wealth of documentary material and analysis. In spite of all the background information and the operative conditions, the play takes its ground from ". . . the proposition that for every man there is a choice, and even by avoiding making that choice, he is in fact choosing" (preface). The clear narratorial conclusion emerging from the presentation of the evidence is that the wrong choice was made. According to Hochhuth, the Vatican leaders were in a strong position, and could have exerted moral authority. Instead, they chose to defend their own immediate interests—to protect the Vatican itself, rather than to challenge Nazi monstrosity. The author also insists that he has not distorted the historical facts. He argues that ". . . the author of the play has only allowed freedom to his imagination when it was necessary to transform the available historical raw material into a form suitable for the stage. The truth has always been respected, but the sediment has been removed" ("Historical sidelights," p. 269).

A much more ambiguous moral judgment emerges from Yehoshua Sobol's play, *Ghetto*.[30] It is not surprising that this should be so, as what comes under investigation here is mainly the behavior of the victims rather than that of the oppressors. We are in the Vilna ghetto in the years 1942–43, and the Jews have to respond to Nazi occupation. Should they cooperate with the ruling power in the hope of saving more lives, or should they resist? And if they resist, should the resistance be violent or peaceful? Different propositions are presented by the various protagonists involved in the creation of the Yiddish theatre in the ghetto. The partisans (led by Yitzhak Wittenberg, Joseph Glazman, and Abba Kovner) are in the background, refusing all collusion. In the foreground are Jacob Gens, chief of the Jewish police, who was appointed Head of the Ghetto in July 1942 and who promoted cooperation, and Hermann Krook, librarian and spokesman for the Socialist Bund, who rejected the idea. The main source for the information in the play is *The Diary of the Vilna Ghetto* (in Yiddish) by Yitzhok Rudashevski, but the focus on the theatre allows the author to project the conflict and the differences of approach. In hindsight, we know that, pragmatically, the debate was futile. Whether the Jews were passive or aggressive, cooperative or rebellious, socialist or Zionist, the outcome would no doubt have remained the same. When so much force is applied and when the aggressor holds all the cards—armed forces, populations, governments—any movement of resistance is illusory, and collaboration futile. It is the illusion of one cast from a top-story window who imagines that he can influence the direction of the fall. But there is still a life beyond the drama itself, and Jewish life can be asserted beyond the war, historically and geographically.[31] A note of defiance can intervene in an otherwise desperate situation. In any event, Sobol's play eschews facile emotionalism by the defamiliarizing effects of song and character transitions, by theoretical debates about behavior and the nature of Jewry, and by the introduction of the grotesque. The author moves in and out of history. Ironic counterpoint is also deployed, as when the Nazi, Dr. Paul, compares his sudden arrival in the ghetto to Yohanan ben Zakkai's move to Yavne. The audience is aware that ben Zakkai's aim was to redeem the Jewish heritage, whereas Dr. Paul's was to pluck it out by the roots.

The Second Generation and Israel

The possible ways of looking at the Holocaust are manifold. There are the events themselves, the experience of the victims, the experience of the oppressors. There are the survivors, the witnesses, and those who receive the story. We can speculate about the causes and the aftermath. It is inevitable, too, that one growing concern will be the effect on the second generation and beyond. How is the message to be received and transmitted further, and what are the behavioral effects?

Such questions are raised by young writers, and they are particularly an issue in Israel. The connection between Israel and the Holocaust cannot be doubted, although it would be dangerous to argue, as many do, that Israel owes its existence to the annihilation of European Jewry. But ideologically, Israel presents some sort of answer. Powerlessness becomes empowerment; the obliteration of Jewishness is countered by a Hebrew renaissance. Jewish typology is stood on its head. In Israel, young writers are taking up the subject. Savyon Liebrecht focuses on the generational conflict, and invokes the subject as a generational labeling device in the stories

"Doves" and "Hayuta's Engagement Party."[32] In "Cutting," too, Granny Henya imposes her obsessions, drawn from the world "out there," on her granddaughter.[33]

Nava Semel's collection of stories, *Kova zekhukhit,*[34] deals almost exclusively with the experiential meeting between two generations. When a direct link is not made between the Holocaust and the plot, an oblique reference to the parents' experience is often made. The generation of the parents bears not only the memory, but also behavior patterns, from the past. The constant switches between the first-person narrator and the third-person narrated indicate this self-identification. The persons in the stories do not escape the experience, and sometimes they, as in the story "Epilogue," deliberately seek out renewed contact with the experience. In this story, the narrator visits Auschwitz and hears someone explain that he comes to the site of the camp because "Auschwitz has charged the batteries of the long years of my life." Although it is the experience of the mother that is at issue, the daughter needs to know it in order to understand herself. So she internalizes it as well as she can, and makes her own pilgrimage to the site.

Summary

We have not been dealing here with the Holocaust itself, but rather with the way that the story is told. More specifically, we have been looking at the narrative posture, as well as at narrative frameworks and the assumptions made. The difficulty of the subject derives from the oxymoron inherent in the label "Holocaust literature." Literature is art, a device for creating pleasurable effects. Our subject then is the esthetics of horror.

But the word "pleasure" may be misleading. Our pleasure in reading is not of a piece, and what interests us in regard to Holocaust literature is appropriate usage of the event. Not, indeed, one single appropriate usage, but the various ways in which writers can shape the material, while remaining true to history, and thoughtful regarding its transmission. Writers about the Holocaust deal with the most highly charged, but also the most fundamental, material available. An experiment was conducted in stretching evil to its ultimate, and that experiment had as its principal laboratory the Jewish people. But Jews, as well as many others who were victims, persisted beyond the deluge. Some survived and passed on the testimony. Most did not, but evidence of their presence was retained. There are witnesses, witnesses of witnesses, and those who come after, who read and learn.

The types of the literature are so various. There are chronicles, memoirs, reconstructions, imaginative variations on a theme, speculation on the event, tangential narratives, attempts to capture the rhythm of the episode, elegies, concern with the appropriate response, debates on reactive behavior, the paralysis of the aftermath, reflections of the survivor, the knowledge inherited by the second generation, and the consideration of Jewish survival. There are many types of narrator, too, deriving from narrative typology: insider, survivor, witness, outsider, commentator, philosopher. And, of course, there is considerable overlap, so that any single narrative partakes of more than one of these stances. The foci are diverse, and so the narratives differ. We cannot assign legitimacy to any one genre over another. The most we can do is to describe the way each work functions within a genre, as a type of one genre, but also as related to others. The success of the implementation is to be judged by the reader.

Notes

1. Elie Wiesel, "For Some Measure or Humility," *Shema,* October 1975.
2. T. W. Adorno, "Engagement," *Noten zur Literatur 3* (Frankfurt: Suhrkamp, 1965), p. 109.
3. See Alvin Rosenfeld's projection of the subject: "As I will argue frequently in the following chapters, it is not warfare in general or even World War II in particular that is of primary concern to the writers of the Holocaust, but Hitler's *Endlosung,* and that considered less as 'theme' than grasped as a major turning point in history and the history of consciousness." *A Double Dying* (Bloomington: Indiana University Press, 1980), p. 10.
4. See Lawrence Langer, *The Holocaust and the Literary Imagination* (New Haven: Yale University Press, 1975), and Rosenfeld, op. cit., pp. 29–34.
5. Rosenfeld, op. cit. p. 68.
6. *Bet haBubot* (Tel-Aviv, 1953, Hebrew); *House of Dolls* (London: Frederick Muller, 1956).
7. *La Douleur* (Paris: P.O.L., 1985; London: Collins, 1986).
8. Ibid., p. 14. My translation.
9. William Styron, *Sophie's Choice* (1976; London: Corgi, 1981).
10. D. M. Thomas, *The White Hotel* (London: Penguin Books, 1981).

11. Anatoli Kuznetzov, *Babi Yar* (New York: Farrar, Straus & Giroux, 1970).

12. The Jewishness on her father's side had been totally rejected. Consequently, she is described as feeling "not in the slightest degree Jewish" (p. 113). This is as reported by the fictionalized Freud in the "case history" of section 3.

13. Richard L. Rubenstein, *The Cunning of History* (New York: Harper Colophon, 1975).

14. See William Styron, *The Confessions of Nat Turner* (New York: Random House, 1967).

15. Primo Levi, *If This is a Man* (London: Penguin Books, 1969); first published as *Se questo e un uomo,* Milan, 1958.

16. Oddly enough, Styron notes that ". . . for various reasons the nearby factories produced very little synthetic rubber . . ." (from the introduction to Rubinstein, op. cit. p. 12). No reasonable conclusions are drawn from this remarkable failure to exploit the available labor, with all the conditions so favorable for production.

17. Isaac Bashevis Singer, *Enemies* (New York: Jonathan Cape, 1972); first published in Yiddish in the New York newspaper *Forverts* as *Sonim: di geshikhte fun a liebe,* 1966).

18. Saul Bellow, *Mr. Sammler's Planet* (New York: Weidenfeld & Nicolson, 1969; Penguin edition, 1971, cited here).

19. Saul Bellow, *The Bellarosa Connection* (London: 1989).

20. Elie Wiesel, *La Nuit* (Paris, 1958); *Night* (London: Fontana Books, 1960) is the edition cited here.

21. Ellen S. Fine, *Legacy of Night* (Albany: SUNY Press, 1982), p. 2.

22. Primo Levi, op. cit.

23. This is the title of a posthumously published work, *I sommersi e i salvati.* Turin, 1986. It provides a theoretical reconsideration of the lessons of the camps.

24. *Il tavolo periodico* (Turin, 1975); *The Periodic Table* (London: Abacus, 1984) is the edition cited here.

25. See *The Drowned and the Saved,* p. 12 for an explication of the distinction made between separate categories of inmates, categories which otherwise tend to be blurred.

26. *Il giardino dei Finzi-Contini* (Milan, 1962); *The Garden of the Finzi-Continis* (London: Quartet Encounters, 1989) is the edition cited here.

27. Aharon Appelfeld, *Badenheim 1939* (London: J. M. Dent, 1981). It was first published in Hebrew in *Shanim vesha'ot* (Tel Aviv, 1975).

28. See, for example, *Ha'or vehakutonet* (Tel Aviv, 1971). This is Appelfeld's first long fiction, and it establishes the pattern for his later novellas, which are frequently expansions of the earlier stories.

29. Rolf Hochhuth, *Der Stellvertreter,* first performed in the "Freie Volksbuhne," Berlin, 20 February 1963. Published in the same year in German and English. The edition here cited is *The Representative* (London: Methuen, 1963).

30. Yehoshua Sobol, *Ghetto,* written between 23 February and 4 March 1983, was first performed in Haifa in 1984. The text cited was published in Tel Aviv, 1984.

31. This was particularly stressed in the London production, with a variant selection of songs, including *"Mir Leben Eyviq"* (We'll live forever) and the resurrection at the end. It must be understood that the play changes with each production, and diverges from the original text.

32. Savyon Liebrecht, *Tapuḥim min hamidbar* (Tel Aviv, 1986).

33. "Kritah," in *Susim al kvish gehah* (Tel Aviv, 1968). This volume also in-

cludes "Sonya Musqat," a story set in Bulgaria during World War II; in it a young girl is sent to a village and has an affair there.

    34. Nava Semel, *Kova zekhukhit* (Tel Aviv, 1985).

Works Cited

Adorno, T. W. 1965. "Engagement." *Noten zur Literatur 3*. Frankfurt: Suhrkamp.

Appelfeld, A. 1981. *Badenheim 1939*. London: J. M. Dent.

Appelfeld, A. 1971. *Ha'or vehakutonet*. Tel Aviv: Am Oved.

Bassani, G. 1962. *Il Giardino dei Finzi Contini*. Milan: Giulio Einaudi. 1989. *The Garden of the Finzi-Continis*. London: Quartet Encounters.

Bellow, S. 1969. *Mr. Sammler's Planet*. New York: Weidenfeld & Nicolson.

Bellow, S. 1989. *The Bellarosa Connection*. London: Secker & Warburg.

Duras, M. 1985. *La Douleur*. Paris: P.O.L., 1986. London: Collins.

Fine, E. S. 1982. *Legacy of Night*. Albany: SUNY Press.

Hochhuth, R. 1963. *Der Stellvertreter*. Berlin: Reimbek bei Hamburg. 1963. *The Representative*. London: Methuen.

Ka-Tzetnik 135633. 1953. *Bet habubot*. Tel Aviv: Dvir. 1956. *House of Dolls*. London: Frederick Muller.

Kuznetsov, A. 1970. *Babi Yar*. New York: Farrar, Straus & Giroux.

Langer, L. 1975. *The Holocaust and the Literary Imagination*. New Haven: Yale University Press.

Levi, P. 1958. *Se questo e un uomo*. Milan: Giulio Einaudi. 1979. *If this is a man*. London: Penguin Books.

Levi, P. 1975. *Il tavolo periodico*. Turin: Giulio Einaudi. 1984. *The Periodic Table*. London: Abacus.

Levi, P. 1986. *I sommersi e i salvati*. Turin: Giulio Einaudi. 1988. *The Drowned and the Saved*. London: Penguin Books.

Liebrecht, S. 1986. *Tapuḥim min hamidbar*. Tel Aviv: Sifriat Poalim.

Liebrecht, S. 1988. *Susim al kvish gehah*. Tel Aviv: Laor.

Rosenfeld, A. 1980. *A Double Dying*. Bloomington: Indiana University Press.

Rubenstein, R. 1975. *The Cunning of History*. New York: Harper Colophon.

Semel, N. 1985. *Kova zekhukhit*. Tel Aviv: Sifriat Poalim.

Singer, I. B. 1972. *Enemies*. New York: Jonathan Cape.

Sobol, Y. 1984. *Ghetto*. Tel Aviv: Or Am.

Styron, W. 1967. *The Confessions of Nat Turner*. New York: Random House Corgi.

Styron, W. 1976. *Sophie's Choice*. New York: Random House Corgi.

Thomas, D. M. 1981. *The White Hotel*. London: Penguin Books.

Wiesel, E. 1958. *La nuit*. Paris: Editions de Minuit. 1960. *Night*. London: Fontana Books.

The Ivory Tower and the Gas Chamber: On the Nature and Teaching of Holocaust Literature

ABRAHAM MARTHAN

Holocaust Literature—The Uses of Incongruity

The joining of these two words together raises at the outset several questions about the relation of literature to life and society in general. The word "Holocaust" is probably the most charged word in the vocabulary of the twentieth century. One who is attempting to write about it, not to say one who is trying to teach it, is gripped with a sense of awesome responsibility. How can literature, with the fragile and delicate means at its disposal, and with certain presuppositions about its own nature and character, handle a subject that demands involvement, identification, even judgment? Also, from the point of view of the potential learner or student, there is bound to be a difference of attitude toward the subject from the very beginning. For this pair of words, *Sifrut Ha'shoa,* this "construct" expression, so to speak, is so very different from similarly constructed expressions like "love literature," etc. We can safely assume that one contemplating enrolling in such courses as the above, is primarily interested in aesthetic pleasure: how poets perceive, feel, or even celebrate the subjects of love or nature, through their use of the agency of words and by means of the wealth of imagery at their disposal. In the normal course of things, the student's expectation is to derive artistic pleasure from such an experience alongside, of course, some degree of understanding of human nature, or the nature of the world. However, in our case, we may safely assume that one contemplating taking a course in Holocaust literature, is of an entirely different mind-set altogether, and that aesthetic pleasure as such is probably the furthest thing from the intention of such a person. Rather, the main motive probably deals with the human, social and moral aspect of the subject: how did it happen, and why did it happen, and what can we learn from it.

This pair of words seems to be joined together in an uncomfortable relationship, to say the least. Some have called the expression "Holocaust literature" a contradiction in terms. These words test each other, as no other similarly constructed expression does. Their close proximity, their "neighborliness," their being together and forming one pair, raise enormous questions. For the Holocaust is primarily an historical, social, human and public phenomenon, while literature, at least as we have been trained to see it in the Western tradition, is an aesthetic and personal category. But it is here precisely that an opportunity arises, and it is to this that I wish to call attention, rather than to the contrariness of the terms. Since no other subject raises the issue of the relationship of life, society, and morality to literature as this subject does, may not this fact itself be a challenge to us, by forcing us to examine the more deeply the nature of each, and the character of their relationship? Instead of seeing this situation as immobilizing—some have advised silence but not kept it—should we not respond by seizing the opportunity to ponder in depth the ultimate relation of life to literature and perhaps rethink the nature of both, their mutualities and responsibilities? Any answer, if there is any, or any position that we arrive at, may help illuminate the relation of literature to society in general. Insights garnered here, from the extremity of the human condition, may be of relevance to other more conventional themes of literature.

Harry Wolfson has said that real philosophical thinking was born only as Greek philosophy encountered religious faith. Out of the clash of faith and reason flew the sparks of philosophical thought. That is why he accorded Philo such a prominent place in the history of philosophy, making him the fountainhead of all subsequent religious philosophical thought, whether Jewish, Christian, or Moslem, and that is why, in his opinion, medieval philosophy is the crown jewel of intellectual enterprise. May we not say the same thing as regards our own subject, and see the relationship of literature to Holocaust not only as a troubled one, but as a creative relationship as well? The juxtaposition of reason and faith helped each illuminate the other, helped each define and clarify itself, made each *aware* of its own nature. The juxtaposition of literature and the Holocaust may do the same thing.

Expressing the Inexpressible: The Insufficiency of Language

It is claimed that such a catastrophe as the Holocaust is unprecedented, that the enormity of the disaster has disrupted the normal means of expression, violated all codes, confused all signals. The strings of the ordinary human lyre, so to speak, have ruptured. Yet this is precisely what the author of the Book of Lamentations claimed: "What can I take as a witness or liken to you, O fair Jerusalem? What can I match with you to console you, O fair maiden Zion? For your ruin is as vast as the sea, who can heal you?" (2:13). Let us put ourselves in the mind-set of a Hebrew person living at the time. The destruction of God's temple by a heathen enemy was unprecedented, and according to the then-prevailing theology (*not* Jeremiah's), an idea so absolutely inconceivable as to border on heresy. What *mashal* can be given to such a calamity? asks the poet. For it is itself a *mashal,* to serve in the future as the ultimate example of disaster. (U. Z. Greenberg says the same thing regarding the Holocaust.) Yet, we must note that this in itself is a *verbal* statement; the silence sought is literarily framed, like the meaningful silences in musical composition. The poet did not give up the attempt to express, or even to "match" the event. But he went ahead to tell the story, fully aware of the insufficiency of the accepted literary convention, simulating horror by use of *mashal.* In fact, in the very same verse, after exclaiming "What can I match with you," he goes on and uses a simile anyhow: "For your ruin is as vast as the sea" *(ka-yam).* Poets continue to try to "catch up" to the real horror of history, continue to struggle for expression, and push further the limits of the expressible; that is, they continue to do what they know how to do best: make comparisons. (No wonder ancient biblical bards were known as *moshelim.*) Figurative language is one of the most ancient and well-nigh indispensable tools of the poet. Even now, in spite of all the vows, very few have been able to do without it completely, or have been able to keep their vow only to a very limited extent.

As for the "silence" that has been urged repeatedly, it has been more honored in the breech. One is overwhelmed by the volume of such verbal admonitions. Since to the modern man literature has taken the place of ritual, we have lost the right kind of proportion to be allotted to either silence or speech, for *both* are necessary. In the traditional mourning rituals, there are instances in which silence is the proper mode, and others in which it is a necessity, indeed a *duty* to speak. The varying behavior of Job's friends as dictated by the occasion, is a case in point.

We constantly see how the Psalmist reproaches God for his silence and urges him to speak out, that is, to react: "O God, do not be silent" (83:2). The miracle is that God's voice is still alive in man, that he is still able to protest, and remind God of his duty to do so. That is a gift. The very attempt to write is a stab against futility. The very urge to write is to break out of futility, either to express or to make contact. Otherwise, the act of writing will be self-contradictory. If words are our prison, they are also our only means of liberation.

Now, these very formulations—"expressing the inexpressible" or "describing the indescribable"—are either meaningless or are functional in some way. First, they seem to be opaque or self-contradictory statements. For if something is truly inexpressible, then it cannot be expressed, and any attempt to do so must be abandoned at the outset. Alternately, if it can be expressed, it is not really inexpressible. What such a formulation can mean in the context of the Holocaust is, I imagine, that up to now it has not been possible, or even necessary, to express such a thing, because such a thing has never occurred before. But since it has been expressed, it is no longer "inexpressible." Or, that by "inexpressible" we really mean something that is morally reprehensible and humanly unacceptable. Or, we might regard such formulations as literary devices in themselves, trying to impress us with the extraordinary or unprecedented nature of the events which are about to be broached, driving home knowledge of the fact that such a thing has never happened before. In other words, when the poet says there can be no comparison, *mashal,* for such a situation, or that there are no words to express this phenomenon, this in itself is a literary convention, an artistic device, to impress upon us the singularity, the one-time character of the event, and to elicit from us a greater emotional response to this particular disaster than to previously encountered disasters. We have shown this to be the case in Lamentations. The question is whether we may also apply this particular use to Holocaust literature. We are too close, and too shocked by the events, to judge. Will further generations, distanced from our own experience but hopefully still deeply concerned, view these confessions of "inexpressibility" or inadequacy of language, as part and parcel of the rhetoric of the *shoah,* as we are inclined to view the rhetoric of the literary expression of previous disasters?

Let me give a happier example from the prayer *Nishmat.* The poet avers the inability of human language to utter God's praise. He says, "Were our mouth filled with the song of the sea, and our tongue with the ringing praise as the raging waves; were our lips full of adoration as the wide expanse of heaven and our eyes sparkling like the sun or the moon; were our hands spread out in the prayer as the eagles of the sky and our feet as swift as the deer— we should still be unable to thank Thee and bless Thy Name, Lord our God and God of our fathers, for one thousandth of the countless millions of favors which Thou hast conferred on our fathers and on us." Meanwhile, the poet's performance has exceeded his self-declared limits, for he has actually penned a most magnificent hymn to the Creator, based on the poet's stated limitation of ability to do justice to such an undertaking. Hence, the limited means served not to diminish the subject, but to make appreciation that much greater.

So much for classical rhetoric. Could that be the case here also? One is aware that these confessions of the inadequacy of language to express the horror are used to magnify our own feeling for the horror. Yet one is reluctant to use a term such as the "rhetoric of horror." One hopes the the Holocaust has not become literature to such an extent. The motive for our inhibition in this case is not primarily aesthetic, but springs from deeper moral and human grounds.

At present we can only say that one way to deal with the enormity of the Holocaust is not to try to match it, because we shall then ascend the heights of pathos which are sure to be counterproductive, but rather to try to cope with it by means of under-statement.

Teaching the Holocaust

TEACHING THE CHILDREN

Children,
Today we offer you
the Holocaust.

Here are the bodies here
The bunkers here the young
Who were the guards.

We offer you
dear children
this package.

It may go off
in your hands if
you open it hastily

or later
if you set it aside.

—Myra Sklarew, "Teaching the Children," *From the Backyard of the Diaspora* (Washington D.C./San Francisco: Dryad Press, 1976, 1981), p. 34

Perhaps in no other subject matter do the didactic and the aesthetic aspects of the literature impinge so much upon one another as they do in Holocaust literature. This is expecially true when we attempt *teaching* this literature to a constituency still in the formative years of their lives and character, for the question of value—moral, social, and aesthetic—naturally inheres in the teaching of the subject. Also, perhaps in no other subject that we teach in the field of Jewish Studies must we consider the *effect* of what we teach on our audience. In a way we feel a kind of responsibility for the effects of our teaching on the mind and soul and even on the behavior of our students, beyond the strictly academic.

Plato considered the effect of music and poetry on the citizens of his republic. I doubt whether any one of us is ready to accept Plato's answer, but we are not free not to ponder the question. Sometimes there is a feeling that one is treading on broken glass, as Myra Sklarew's poem makes clear.

What the Holocaust has done in this case, is to confound the accepted functions of literature to "delight and instruct." In what way can literary expression of the Holocaust be said to "delight" (heeding Adorno's warning lest we squeeze a drop of pleasure from human suffering)? As for "instruction," what is that we want to learn? Or, for that matter, is it possible to learn from the literature of the Holocaust? Should we then not teach Holocaust literature, or for that matter, the Holocaust at all? The question seems strange, especially after almost half a century of just such an activity; for academics, this is purely an academic question.

Yet it is exactly the position that a noted British historian and university professor, Lionel Kochan, has taken. Backing up what to him was "the most anguished question" of his career, he argues as follows:

> I see the twin perils ahead, one general and one particular. The first derives from the fact that with the Holocaust a threshold was crossed. It may or may not be unique—it is horrendous enough without that classification to show what can be "achieved" and incur the bare minimum of penalty. In our generation it sets a precedent insofar as it is incorporated into the history of the period. What has once happened, can happen twice. The unthinkable has become not only thinkable but also actual.
>
> What applies in general has a particular relevance to the Jews. They are, by common consent, the natural and inevitable victims of persecution. For all sorts of reasons, the image that belongs to the Jews is that of victim, sufferer, martyr, witness. Therefore, to talk of the Holocaust is to reinforce an existing image, to render it more credible, acceptable and—I hate to say it—legitimate. I repeat—though it may be controversial, the less said about the Holocaust the better. And to institute separate "Holocaust Studies" seems to me monstrous. (*AJS Newsletter*, Fall, 1989)

I do not think that, while sharing the above concerns, we want to go this far. An extreme prohibition is neither desirable nor possible. First of all, it is something that *did* happen in full light of history. The knowledge of it can neither be denied nor swept under the rug. It is too important, even central, in both world and Jewish history, to be ignored. It has affected both present and future generations to an incalculable degree. The danger of it happening again is very real, as Professor Kochan correctly notes. But for that very reason, one can argue that it *should* be taught. The social climate in other countries may be different, but certainly from an American perspective, it seems that Professor Kochan's position is too extreme. It is, moreover, fraught with much more danger, for the very reasons that he states, than the opposite view. He is concerned only with one aspect of the case, that it may also do the same *if it is set aside* as poet Myra Sklarew fears.

I think most of us have made the choice that the Holocaust, and its literature, should indeed be taught. The question is, *how?* Should there be any criteria for selection? Are there any priorities? I think that whenever we undertake to teach any subject, we make some choices or judgments, whether explicit or implicit. I think, indeed, that there ought to be some *prerequisites:* at the very least a course in Jewish history or literature other than in the Holocaust area, especially as some of these students are non-Jews, well-intentioned, but ill-prepared for the most part (not that our own Jewish students are well-prepared, but there still is a difference). A course such as Holocaust literature or Holocaust history, dealing as it does with a very complicated and sensitive issue, does need preparation, perhaps a great deal more than we can possibly offer. The student is going to be conducted through the "valley of tears" of Jewish history—in a sense through the "holy of holies," the Jewish people's most sacred as well as most vulnerable spot—and it cannot be done without adequate preparation, regardless of the goodwill, seriousness, and enthusiasm of the potential student.

When we come to the teaching itself, and the texts, I do not think that it is possible to jump to the literature of the Holocaust without providing a context in terms of Hebrew literature itself. Perhaps we ought to include something from the Bible, a chapter from the Book of Lamentations, some selected Psalms, and some post-biblical readings such as the story of Hannah and her seven children for example, the Ten Martyrs, and some illustrative readings from Bernfeld's *The Book of Tears* dealing with materials from the Crusades and the Spanish expulsion. Some selections from modern Hebrew literature *prior* to the Holocaust must also be included: Bialik's *The City of Slaughter* (1903), and Tchernikhovsky's *Ballads of Worms* (1942) at the very minimum, and if possible, Shneur's "The Middle Ages Draw Near" (1913)—at least in parts if not completely. Of course there may not be enough time in one single semester (which is usually the case) to "cover" or do justice to all of these materials. But we have no choice. This kind of enterprise must be done properly or not be done at all. We cannot afford to have the student come out of such a course confused, ill-informed or, worse still, with a negative attitude toward the whole affair.

We also must deal with the Jewish communities not just at the time that they were caught by the cruel events. We must teach what their lives were like *before* the catastrophe struck—their manner of living, their traditions, culture and art, song and dance, the sights and sound, their very voices before they were stifled. We must show the beauty, the character, the human qualities of what was lost.

I would like to illustrate the above point by passages from the lament of Eliezer bar-Judah of Worms (c.1165–c.1230) over the martyrdom of his wife and daughters in 1197, following the events of the Third Crusade (1189–92).

THE MURDER OF BELLET AND HANNAH

> *Let me tell the story of my eldest*
> *daughter, Bellet: She was thirteen*
> *years old, and as chaste as a bride. She*
> *had learnt all the prayers and songs*
> *from her mother, who was modest and*
> *kind, sweet and wise. The girl took*
> *after her beautiful mother and every*
> *night she would make my bed and take*
> *off my shoes. She did her housework*
> *quickly and always spoke the truth.*
> *She worshipped her Maker, she weaved*
> *and sewed and embroidered [in His*
> *Honor], she was filled with reverence*
> *and pure love for her Creator. For the*
> *sake of Heaven, she sat down by me to*
> *hear my teaching. And that is when she*
> *and her mother and her sister were*

*killed, on the night of the twenty-
second of Kislev, as I was sitting peace-
fully at my table. Two wicked men
broke in and killed them before my
eyes; they also wounded me and my
students, and my son.*

*Now let me tell the story of my younger
daughter [Hannah]; every day she
would recite the first portion of the
Shema. She was six years old, and she
knew to weave and sew and embroider
and to delight me with her singing.*
　　—*The Penguin Book of Hebrew Verse*, ed. T. Carmi
　　(New York: Jewish Publication Society/Viking Press,
　　1981), pp. 387–88

This poem makes us feel what was lost. From the enormity and impersonality of the Crusades we are introduced to the private study of Eliezer bar-Judah. We get acquainted with the beautiful souls of these blameless girls. We are completely at one with the grieving father. We feel a genuine sorrow at the loss. The simplicity of the poem stirs our heart the more profoundly. We feel the pain deeply.

Anyone immersed in such texts, shall talk no more of the "banality of evil." This poem does not speak to the twelfth century only, but to our own century as well. It puts the recent Jewish Holocaust in a historical as well as a literary context, and fortifies the process of identification with what is being expressed in the text.

In teaching Holocaust literature we must aspire to the *synoptic* view that binds all generations of Israel. We must not study that literature in isolation, cut off from the rest of Jewish literature or history, but pay attention to the Jewish literary response to suffering and persecution throughout the ages. Indeed, this is immanent in the literary genre of this subject itself. For very often the poets see a recent catastrophe in terms of previous ones—the expulsion from Spain in terms of the destruction of the Second Temple, for example. They call their various persecutors Pharaohs, or Hamans, or they themselves refer to earlier martyrdoms and disasters that have overtaken the Jewish people. Bialik first called his poem "The City of Slaughter" (1903) by the name "The Burden of Nemerov"; everyone knew that he was referring to 1648–49. In his *Baruch of*

Mayence (1901) Tchernikhovsky framed his own response to the pogroms of the early twentieth century in terms of the Crusades. The American-born Israeli poet, Reuven ben-Yosef, mentions in one single poem the names of Nemerov, Uman, Worms, Mayence, Strasbourg, Blois, Seville, and Valencia. Uri Zvi Greenberg very often does the same. The knowledge of these events and the literary response to them is necessary to the understanding of contemporary literature on the Holocaust. More important than the chronologies is the grasp of the essential sensibility and philosophy pervading this literature, namely, the *simultaneity* of Jewish experience. It is remarkable how the most contemporary Hebrew writers, including the native-born, are imbued with this sense of continuity (Gouri, Trainin, Schutz, not to speak of Amichai and Pagis). This sense must be somehow communicated to the student, or else we have not done a complete job.

Hebrew Literature After the Holocaust

I think you can safely say that Hebrew literature in the wake of the Holocaust is not what it was before it, or more precisely, before the lessons of the Holocaust actually sank in. I am thinking in particular about Israeli literature of the War of Independence and the years immediately following. Israeli literature *now* is not what it was in the generation of the Independence. "Elik was born from the sea," proclaimed Moshe Shamir in his novel *With His Own Hands* (1954), a fictionalized account of the life of his younger brother, Elik, who was killed in Israel's War of Independence. The new breed of Israeli Jew would transcend millennia of suffering and victimization, be totally new and owe nothing to his or her predecessors. This is the myth of the "Super-Sabra," so to speak. The change may be due partly to the Eichman trial, which conveyed knowledge and publicized the Holocaust on the popular level; but in literature, it was most assuredly an *internal* matter, and perceptible already by the mid-fifties. Amichai used elements of his life from across the sea, and kept referring to his father and mother and his lost legacy. Haim Gouri was on a mission to the Jewish refugee camps even before the War of Independence, and wrote of his encounter with the refugees, an experience which culminated in his now famous poem "Heritage," ending with the unforgettable line referring to Isaac's offspring: "They are born with a knife in their heart." Later on, the literary creations of child survivors such as Appelfeld and Pagis, and the "Teheran children" such as Benzion Tomer, put their own unique experiences into story, poem and play, and placed their works permanently on the map of Israeli literature. One now looking at the current literary scene in Israel meets such names as David Schutz, David Grossman, and Yehiel Hoffman, and one gets the distinct impression that the leading voices in contemporary literature in Israel are either survivors or children of survivors. They have been stamped by their experience and for one reason or another feel compelled to give legitimacy to their own, or their parents', experience.

However, if we take a further look at the chief literary spokesmen of what has been called the generation of the War of Independence, or the Palmach generation, we see how artificial that stance was at the outset. Let us take, for instance, what came to be a sort of bible of that generation, the anthology *Dor Ba-Aretz*. The name itself is based on a quotation from the poem "I Believe" by Saul Tchernikhovsky. If we take a close look at this collection, we see that it contains the work of some thirty-three writers, about evenly divided between poetry and prose works. Of these writers, fully eighteen of them—over one-half—were born in the Diaspora and brought their memories with them: Gilead, Gilboa, Kovner, Tennai, Tammuz, Aharon and Matti Megged, Mar, the Seneds, Galai, Nitzan, Vered, Shaham (David), Yonatan, Amichai, Hendel, Carmi.

It is true that some of the above were brought to Israel as children, but many of them were teenagers, some of them quite adult when they migrated (Gilboa, Kovner, the Seneds, Carmi), some of them arriving at the very eve of the War of Independence. Thus, the myth of *dor ba-aretz,* the generation of the land, was not true, even at the very beginning, neither as a matter of biographical fact, nor as to the character of many of these writers or their writings. The Diaspora-born authors like Hendel, Gilboa, Kovner, Amichai, Carmi, and some of the native-born such as Tabib and Shahar, identified with historical Jewish experience right from the beginning. The identity of *Dor Ba-Aretz* was purely an act of the will, a Nietzschean resolve for a radical transformation, that was later to be modified beyond recognition. It was possibly a self-elected image, a mask or a persona, donned by some of these writers. Probably it was a result of editorial policy. For the works selected were not completely representative of the works of the writers. Preference was given to works depicting the War of Independence, or kibbutz life and other areas of native Israeli experience. There was nothing of Amichai's Diaspora memories. The poems of Gouri depicting his encounters in Europe with refugees of the Holocaust *predate* his poems of the War of Independence, but nothing of these appear in *Dor Ba-Aretz*. Of the three editors themselves, two were born in the Diaspora!

We know that many of these writers went on to give expression to the life of their ancestors in the Diaspora. Some of them have specifically written about the *shoah,* or its ramifications and effects in Israeli life. Prose writers of *Dor Ba-Aretz* who have been anthologized in *shoah* collections include A. Megged, Bartov, Amichai, Gouri, Ben-Amotz, Yonat and Alexander Sened. Of the poets of *Dor Ba-Aretz,* Gilead, Gilboa, Kovner, Galai, Gouri, Carmi, Amichai and Treinin have made important contributions to *shoah* literature.

What is even more remarkable is that even the poets known as the Generation of the State, such as Ravikovitch, Wieseltier, M. Govrin and Y. Ben-Dor, among others, have added their own distinctive voices to the poetry of the *shoah.*

What accounts for this change? As the temporary intoxication and euphoria induced by the truly amazing victory of the War of Independence waned, a sober mood set in. In the aftermath came the realization that the War of Independence was not the last war, and that the young people of the country were to fight again and again for their own survival as well as for the survival of the state. The establishment of the state did not solve the problem of anti-Semitism, as was envisaged by the Zionist dreamers. Anti-Semitism lived on under other names; ironically, this time the state became its new focus. The awareness of how fragile Jewish existence was everywhere, including in the independent and sovereign state of Israel, brought a deeper, fairer, and more balanced understanding of Jewish life in the Diaspora. An ex-"Canaanite" like Binyamin Tammuz began to see "heroic" dimensions in the daily struggle of the Jew in the Diaspora for survival and maintenance of his or her own identity. The Israeli experience of constant exposure to danger and eternal vigilance in defense of precious life was assimilated into general Jewish experience, as forming a *continuum,* rather than a break. This change was also helped by the coming of age of the children of the survivors, who inherited their parents' memories and sought to give them literary expression. To a great extent the Israeli condition has become emblematic of the Jewish condition, all rolled into one and expressed in terms of *akeda*—as in Haim Gouri's poem "Heritage" already referred to, in a great many *akedot* written by poets who are survivors or children-of-survivors, and also by native Israeli poets. There probably have not been as many *akedot* written since the times of the Crusades as have been written in the forty years of the state's existence. This says something about the sense of Jewish identity of the contemporary Israeli writers, and the ethos of the state as it crystalized in the decades following independence. It is not by accident that both Pagis and Yaoz-Kest saw the dangers of the 1973 war in terms of the *shoah.* Alternately, "exile" has become the Israeli condition. Unfortunately, there is nothing "abnormal" today about the condition of exile; everyone is "alienated" or in "exile"—including Israelis. The Jew as well as the Israeli has become Everyman. This post-independence sensibility was assimilated into the new poetics of the mid-fifties and the prose fiction of the sixties.

Literature after Auschwitz: Some Lessons

The question whether there can be literature after Auschwitz has been asked many times, and various answers have been given. The crime of Auschwitz was so enormous in its scale, totality, thoroughness, technological efficiency, and calculated scientism coupled with the most barbaric fanaticism, that it completely disrupted our normal moral, social and aesthetic standards. It has been asked whether literature, art, or, for that matter, culture as such, is possible. Statements were made that after Auschwitz it was not possible to write poetry. Adorno's objection to poetry after Auschwitz is that art transforms its subject and that a drop of pleasure may be squeezed out of human suffering. That the pain suffered at Auschwitz may yield aesthetic pleasure when transformed into art is of course unthinkable. Yet, here we are almost half a century after Auschwitz, and life goes on. Literature, poetry, and art are still flourishing, and some of it is very good indeed; some of it is about the Auschwitz experience; and some of that too is good literature and good poetry. So what do we make of this situation?

The question should be rephrased. The question is not whether poetry is possible after Auschwitz, for emphatically that has proven to be the case, but whether it is possible to write poetry in the same fashion as *before* Auschwitz. The answer is evidently no. Some changes have to be made regarding our expectations of both life and literature. Some of the writings in world literature, and even in our own field of Hebrew letters, may today sound puerile, irresponsible, even dangerous, in the light of what we know about Auschwitz.

What we can say is that, after Auschwitz, life cannot be the same. The idea of "art for art's sake," never popular with the Hebrews, must be abandoned. A sense of responsibility must be restored to the Word. There must be once more a sense of moral rigor to artistic expression (the prevalence of the "Hebraic" over the "Hellenic" ideal in Arnold's terms, or the synthesis of both as indicated by Tchernikhovsky?). The idea of the "ivory tower," or the absolute autonomy of art, is no longer tenable, no more than is the autonomy of business. Very few of us today would subscribe to the idea that "the business of business is business," regardless of the larger social consequences. We are no longer able to say with Eliot that poetry is a superior form of amusement. The ivory tower must recognize its responsibility to the gas chamber. Literature must be restored once more to its biblical task of criticism of life—at least this should be one of its main tasks. If saving a life overrides the commandment of the Torah, i.e. suspends the claim of religion, then certainly human life is to be held superior to the sanctity of art. Regard for human life must override the claims of art.

On the other hand, we must cherish the value of literature and art and must guard against the ever-present danger of censorship. The danger is always there, ready to be applied by the vulgar under the pretense of moral uprightness. Poetry must go on after Auschwitz, otherwise we shall be handing the Nazis another victory. What has changed probably forever is our way of looking at and teaching literature. Separating the idea of the reality and pleasure of literature from its human consequences and implications, must be given up. We must take a firm stand on the matter and plant ourselves squarely on biblical grounds. The Hebrew prophets ought to be our ideal. They were supreme poets, and yet they were imbued with moral pathos; they "translated ethical passion into verse" (E. Silberschlag). The majesty of speech and power of moral ardor in Isaiah and Elijah's rebuke to Ahab following the latter's takeover of Naboth's vineyard—"Would you murder and take possession?"—(1 Kings 21:19), should be our guides. The moral indignation of Isaiah, the spiritual earnestness of the Psalms, their insistent pursuit of ultimate justice, did not prevent those books from becoming masterpieces of world literature. On the contrary, it is the moral stance behind the words that contributed to their artistic merit. The biblical writers held to the ideals of both high art and high morality.

We must *not* compromise on artistic standards. In choosing a piece of literature dealing with the Holocaust, or any Jewish topic for that matter, we must insist on high artistic merit. A poem, a short story, or a novel cannot slide by on the merit of its subject matter alone. The rigors of literary criteria applied elsewhere must apply here too. *There can be no compromise with artistic quality.* Human conscience cannot afford to express itself in a less artistic voice than ordinary writings do. Should the Shulamite be less beautiful than Helen of Troy? She can be good and beautiful at the same time! (The "artistic" must not be confused with the "artificial"—on the contrary!) We must be careful not to create one aesthetic category for Holocaust literature and another for everything else. In doing so we shall be conceding a very important value to the enemy.

Fortunately, a literature dealing with the Holocaust combines ultimate horror with superior artistic expression exists in the Hebrew language. The works of Appelfeld, Schutz, Grossman, U. Z. Greenberg, Amichai, Pagis, among many others, come most clearly to mind. They provide incontestable evidence of the triumph both of the human spirit and of the artistic impulse.

Does Holocaust Literature Possess Universal Import?

I have saved the most controversial question for last. This is truly a mine field. This issue is tied to the more basic question of whether the Holocaust is only Jewish. Sometimes the question is stated in terms who "owns" the Holocaust. The historians seem to have invested a great deal of time and energy on this question, but it is of no less interest to those of us whose main focus is literature, and especially the *teaching* of literature. Bear in mind also that many of our students, especially in this course of Jewish Studies, are non-Jews.

While some historians have shied away, as we have seen, from teaching the subject at all, some are equally vehement against all attempts to "de-Judaize" the Holocaust. In what sense is the Holocaust Jewish? Or in what sense is it Jewish only? It is certainly unprecedented, in the sense that it never happened before, whether to a Jew or a non-Jew. It is also incomparable, in the sense that Jewish suffering during the Holocaust exceeded that of other peoples in terms of number, proportion of targeted group, etc. Still all these do not make the Holocaust "Jewish only." *I* grew up on the idea that Hitler was an enemy of humanity, that Nazism was destructive of all culture and freedom as such; that we had magnificent allies in fighting Hitler, such as Churchill, Roosevelt, Stalin, De Gaulle, feisty Swedes and Danes. In the postwar revelations, many of these illusions were shattered. Our own reading of the Holocaust (the prevailing one, that is), tends to isolate Jews from the rest of humanity. We may be falling into the trap set by our enemies. If this calamity happened to "Jews only," why should anybody else care?

This problem is most crucial to us as teachers of literature for, unlike history, literature cannot be taught as a purely academic discipline. It depends a great deal on *empathy,* the ability to identify. Granted that the Holocaust was unique to the Jews, that the Jews bore the brunt of it, that they were singled out for the severest punishment, I still think it is a mistake to limit it exclusively to the Jews. For that leaves us without allies, whether real or imaginary. It creates a distance between Jews and non-Jews, for if the Holocaust is basically a Jewish problem, it is of necessity only of academic interest to the non-Jew. People will say that if this is an exclusively Jewish problem, then it does not touch them; thus the entire literature is rendered completely unteachable, except to Jews. And then it is bound to result in a state of total depression. I think this exclusive emphasis has backfired, and after forty years of Holocaust education, some are trying to deny it.

The power of literature and art is that it can appeal to people across national and religious boundaries. Nazism was, and must be, depicted as an enemy of humanity and civilization wherever they are. It was not only the Jews who were endangered by Hitler and Nazi teachings (this is true, of course, of all totalitarian systems). True, Jews suffered much more than anybody else in the intensity of their persecution and in proportion to noncombatants, but Nazi aggression left millions dead and enormous physical and cultural destruction in its wake. It left Europe in shambles and wrought worldwide havoc. Numbers are not the sole determinants of the damage done. In the final analysis it was Nazi ideology that was inimical to civilization as we know it.

This is a matter of utmost importance to us as teachers of literature. For to be effective we must communicate. Only that which can be shared can be communicated. Only that which can be communicated can be truly appreciated.

As a part and parcel of our teaching of Holocaust literature we could avail ourselves of the writing of anti-Nazi authors and artists who were themselves exiles from their country, such as Thomas Mann and Bertolt Brecht. There were non-Jewish writers even in those dark times who contiued to champion traditional humanistic values, regardless of the sacrifices that their activities entailed. There were philo-Semites and other decent beings, who shared our agonies in the time of our greatest disaster. One of the best and the most significant expressions of this universal sense of shared humanity was captured by W. H. Auden in his poem "The Diaspora."

This poem touches the heart of the matter. It is a powerful statement of moral passion and beauty. It should be included in every syllabus of Holocaust literature for its articulation of the bright side of the human face.

THE DIASPORA

> How he survived them they could never understand:
> Had they not beggared him themselves to prove
> They could not live without their dogmas or their land?
>
> No worlds they drove him from were ever big enough:
> How could it be the earth Unconfined
> Meant when It bade them set no limits to their love?

And he fulfilled the role for which he was designed:
On heat with fear, he drew their terrors to him,
And was a godsend to the lowest of mankind.

Till there was no place left where they could still pursue him
Except exile which he called his Race.
But, envying him even that, they plunged right through him

Into a land of mirrors without time or space,
And all they had to strike now was the human face.
        —The Collected Poetry of W. H. Auden (New York:
        Random House, 1945), pp. 55–56

Memory in the Work of Yehiel Dinur (Ka-Tzetnik 135633)

WILLIAM D. BRIERLEY

Introduction

A shaft of sunlight, long and pointed, broke in through one of the shutter slits, stabbing the centre of the floor like a javelin. Myriad flecks of dust danced in the beam as though newly born with the knowledge that only within its limits could they dance out their obscure lives. Were they to pass beyond it they would cease to be.[1]

Memory is fragile. Like "flecks of dust" the victims of the Holocaust are at risk from the forces which work against it: distortion, revisionism and forgetfulness. Only the survivor, the one who was "over there," can represent those who were lost and act as the shaft of light in which they are preserved.

The sleeve of the Ka-Tzet uniform is ripped to the shoulder. He gazes at the six digits of the Ka-Tzet number on his forearm. The blue outlines of the digits streak before his eyes: a blue river. His arm is the bed of the river. . . . There they live out their lives. All the vast multitudes of them. There, in the river depths, flow his days, his night. Cities of them crowded with Jews, Jewish towns and hamlets.[2]

Ka-Tzetnik 135633 was "over there." Despite his enormous success as a novelist, he is perhaps the most mysterious and critically neglected of all Holocaust writers. Rarely has he stepped out of his anonymity; in June 1961 he gave testimony at the Eichmann trial, though he collapsed before finishing his statement. It was here that the Israeli public learned for the first time that his official name was Yehiel Dinur.[3] His work is not mentioned in almost any of the major English language critical studies of Holocaust literature.[4] It may have been felt that Dinur made such an early and immediate impact, that his work had achieved its purpose and did not merit deeper analysis. If this is true, it is unfortunate, because the four novels and one volume of prose poems available in English translation are sophisticated works of literature, deserving critical attention both as works of witness and works of art. This paper, a study of the theme of memory in Dinur's work, is partly intended to demonstrate the possibility of a critical reevaluation of his work.

"Over There"

The major dilemma of the Holocaust writer is commonly acknowledged to be the struggle to find language with which to convey the "Univers concentrationaire," for "it was a world set apart, utterly segregated, a strange kingdom with its own peculiar fatality."[5] The two halves of the cannot write/must write paradox are clearly evident in Dinur's work. A young woman character, in the twilight zone between liberation and resurrection, voices the despair of language found so often in Holocaust writing:

> There is no one on this earth who can understand us, except ourselves. Only we can understand each other, we who do not talk in the language of speech. But with the others? The outsiders? In what language could we explain to them? What could we say that they could possibly understand?[6]

And yet, the central character of Dinur's four novels, the Auschwitz survivor Harry Preleshnik, feels the full weight of the imperative to remember. Like Dinur, who spoke mystically at the Eichmann trial of his power to sustain himself, which, he said derived from a pledge he had given to the people in Auschwitz,[7] Harry makes a vow:

> They had left him behind on their way to the crematorium. In each one's eyes was the command: Tell it! Do not forget! He had to keep going until he had fulfilled his vow![8]

Three particularly important aspects of Dinur's work which exemplify the otherness of the Holocaust Kingdom of Auschwitz, and therefore highlight the difficulties of finding forms by which to

witness and preserve its memory, are the laws of conduct governing Auschwitz, its language and time.

Dinur presents the camp as another planet on which the different
governing laws were instantly tangible.[9] Brute strength determined
right and wrong, and this strength was determined by the acquisition of a prominent position and the continuous obsession—food:

> This they do know: Abram is right! Because Abram is the one eating
> sausage. . . .[10]

Dinur represents the effects of the different values of the system
upon human relationships. Absolute competition undermines soli-
darity: a new campling is told that "anyone wanting to live here's
got to kill somebody else."[11] Abram, the father of a "Piepel," (a
boy used by the block chiefs for sexual gratification), approves of
the arrangement under the new laws, such that he looks upon the
block chief "like the father of the bride taking delight in his first-
rate son-in-law."[12]

Auschwitz also has its own language, full of the violence of the
system. Even Yiddish is so brutalized as to be familiar and yet
alien to the new arrivals.[13] In addition, everyday language changes
its meaning under the new conditions, as what is signified is altered.
Take, for instance, the common word "latrine":

> All the world knows what latrines are for. Doubtless, that is what they
> were set up for in Auschwitz, too. But here everybody knows that
> "'latrine' means 'stock exchange.'"[14]

The word "latrine" therefore takes on a whole new set of meanings.
It is the underground heart of the camp as the center of the prolific
trade which takes place, and it also becomes a symbol of the function of Auschwitz as a whole. The latrine is the environment of
the Musselmen[15] who are, in a metaphor resembling Richard Rubenstein's theory in *After Auschwitz*, the "shit flushing through the
camp to the crematorium."[16] Symbolically, therefore, the pump of
the latrine becomes the "nocturnal heart of Auschwitz,"[17] the very
reason for its existence. "Latrine" no longer signifies a place on
the periphery of human life for the disposal of excrement, but the
central place.

Dinur also represents the otherness of Auschwitz with reference to time. Auschwitz has a different scheme of time from the world outside. In *Star Eternal,* a survivor returns to his native town and, standing in the street contemplating his Auschwitz tattoo,[18] realizes that

> His own time is utterly divorced from him. Strange: his time flows at once there, within the depths of the blue river of his tatooed Ka-Tzet number, and outside, along Park Street.[19]

In Auschwitz, for the common camplings at least, there is only a hopeless, unbroken mass of time:

> The day already unfurled over Auschwitz. A new Auschwitz day, but familiar in every scent and hue. One just like it was here yesterday, and one just like it will be here tomorrow—after you. Besides it, there is nothing here. Everywhere—Auschwitz.[20]

Normal chronological progression, as well as the "real" time of person and collective, are absent. In *Piepel,* Moni, Harry's little brother, realizes that he does not know how old he is because his birthday is unmarked. Elsewhere, in the same novel, Dinur notes the loss of Jewish calendar time:

> Once it had been Yom Kippur today. Jews had prayed for a good new year. After Yom Kippur had come Sukkot, Simchat Torah. What will come after Yom Kippur this time?[21]

Dinur's alternation from narration in the past tense to the present tense heightens the sense of the loss of time in this, and other, passages.

Just as the witness's struggle with language is represented in the novels, so is the struggle with time. As Harry Preleshnik first attempts to write down his memories, he finds that time stands against him as an enemy:

> No longer were his days divided into measurable units of calendar or clock. Time had become one solid mass, and like an amorphous body it stood opposite him, across the desk, its palm covering the blankness of the notebook page. They looked directly at each other. He and time. Two foes. The death of his past world on the one side; his life in present suspension on the other.[22]

In terms of underlying laws, language and time, the work of

witness is presented in Dinur's work as a process of translation and connection. It is both the translation of Holocaust memories into the concepts, language, and chronology of this world, and the establishment of connections which allow these memories to be encountered and worked through. This is a costly and dangerous process, yet it appears in Dinur's work as an imperative:

> Like drifting smoke, the lesson of Auschwitz will disappear if man does not learn from it. And if Auschwitz is forgotten, man will not deserve to live.[23]

This aspect of his work will be returned to after a consideration of the problems inherent to memory and remembering, as they are seen in Dinur's work.

The Fragility of Memory

In witnessing to the Holocaust, Dinur clearly feels himself to be a mouthpiece for those who did not return. Their memory is constantly threatened by the nature of memory itself and by the forces at work to counter it. He presents the fragility of memory both in the camps and afterward.

Dinur shows how, under the extreme conditions of mental, emotional, and physical deprivation endured by the camplings, memory is obliterated. The struggle to obtain the bare essentials of life is so intense that even a wife or child can be forgotten.[24] When memory does return to a campling, the truth of Dante's dictum that "there is no greater pain than to recall a happy time in times of misfortune" is realized, as in this encounter in *House of Dolls:*

> An indescribable grief now lay on the bony face. Daniella felt guilty, as though her being there had brought it about. Her appearance from the outside world must have reopened forgotten wounds in this poor wretch's heart.[25]

Even a "prominent" could feel the pain of memory, such as the murderous Piotr "Holy Dad" of *Piepel,* who admitted:

> They give me a pain those Piepels . . . they flap around the blocks like butterflies. Green, and still stinking of outside air.[26]

In another episode, Daniella attempts to retain a locket which contains pictures of herself and her brother Moni, as she enters a camp. Like the camplings themselves, her memories contained in this, her "only remembrance,"[27] are reduced to excrement; she is told she may keep it, for "tomorrow you'll throw the shit away yourself."[28] There is no place for memories of the past on the Auschwitz planet, for they either bring despair for the campling or an attack of conscience for the prominent.

The assault upon memory is compounded by the loss of names. In a system designed as an assault upon individuality, the last thing which Harry Preleshnik has stripped from him is his name, the symbol of memory and identity.[29] Its recovery marks the first stage on his road back to life.[30] However, it is clear from Dinur's work that the total loss of individuality does not come at the stage of the campling's loss of his or her name, for here they gain the new identity of a number. As antipersonal as this might seem, the uniqueness of each number in the camp leaves the campling utterly exposed at times of selection. Rather, the total loss of individuality occurs at the "Musselman" stage; Dinur recurrently employs images of the sea or river for this camp group, to convey the complete personal obliteration which has taken place. Thus, when Harry Preleshnik, having become a Musselman, narrowly escapes the gas chamber, the German guards who allow him to live tell him that he is a number and not just another Musselman.[31]

It is perhaps as a result of this loss of name and identity that Dinur emphasizes the importance of both in the world after the Holocaust. The episode concerning the survivor Abrasha, in *House of Love,* is central to this concern. Abrasha escapes from Europe to Palestine with Harry Preleshnik. He has great difficulty adjusting to his new home, which is symbolized by the difficulty he has in mastering Hebrew.[32] Like Harry, Abrasha writes an account of his experiences in wartime Europe where he hid for years in the cesspool of a Polish farm. This account is his testimony to the destruction of his home and family. However, because Harry's book *Salamandra* (here Dinur blurs with his leading protagonist, as *Salamandra* is the original title of *Sunrise Over Hell*) has already been published and has been a great success, the potential publishers of Abrasha's manuscript turn it down.

Harry, who tries to help his friend, is outraged, arguing the case for its uniqueness:

> What is in that manuscript in front of you now could have been written by no one but this man.[33]

Abrasha's fate symbolizes that of those survivors who were unable to find listeners for their testimony. Shortly afterward he dies, neglected and, with the exception of Harry, unmourned. He is carelessly buried in a child's grave and, with no family to preserve it, his memory is wiped away. As Harry looks around the cemetery he reflects upon the tombstones:

> Names. Names. Names. Perpetuating their memories for the living. Abrasha had left no one living behind; not even his name, therefore, would be remembered. He was the last of his family, the last of his town. Now he too was gathered unto them.[34]

Abrasha is forgotten and in his obliteration Auschwitz claims its final victory over him and his family.

Forgetfulness is only one reflection of the fragility of memory in Dinur's work. Another of his major fears is of the distortion of memory, at the heart of which is the issue of who should testify to the Holocaust. Two groups attract his particular attention: the Poles, and Jews who were not in the camps.

Dinur comes from Poland, where his pre-Auschwitz name was Karol Cetynski, and he worked as a journalist.[35] While he never loses sight of the fact that the Poles were also Hitler's victims, he clearly retains great hostility towards the inhabitants of the nation of his birth. He claims that the Poles were so anti-Semitic that their hatred blinded them to the threat which Germany posed:

> The people of Poland, lulled to sleep by anti-Semitic chants, now provided ground for a Fifth Column. Willingly, public opinion let itself be led by the nose. Drunks in Polish army uniforms, swigging vodka as they staggered along the streets, called on Hitler to rid Polish soil of this plague of Jewish vermin.[36]

It is not without a sense of irony that the 'Fifth Column' accusation, once leveled at the Jews, should be turned back upon the Poles.

Within Auschwitz, the Poles are represented as having a considerable advantage over the Jewish camplings. They hold prominent positions, receive food parcels,[37] rarely turn into Musselmen and are 'never' taken away to the crematorium.[38] An anxiety about their presence in the camp is voiced by Haiml-Idl, a major character in *Piepel*. He bitterly resents the way in which the Poles prevent the Jewish prisoners from stealing food from the peelry and remarks:

> After the war those Polacks will show off the numbers on their arms—martyred saints! They were in Auschwitz! The Jews won't be able to show their arms, because Jews there won't be.[39]

Elsewhere in the novel, Haiml-Idl reflects upon Matchek, a murderously brutal Pole, who was the worst Jew-hater amongst the potato peelers:

> After the war Matchek will be "Mr. Auschwitz Campling," the only victim of the Germans.[40]

Dinur provides a counterwitness to what he sees as these distortions of memory. It is worth noting, nevertheless, that while his judgment of the Polish people is far from flattering, he does recognize their victimhood. Even as a Polish *kapo* flogs Moni, Dinur provides a glimpse of the hierarchy of oppression:

> Murderously he flogs away, as though not Moni but the S. S. chief were now lying on the bench, and Vatzek were now venting all his pent-up wrath on him: for his three years in Auschwitz, for the girl he left behind at the village near Zamoszc whom the Germans must now be laying . . .[41]

The second distortion which Dinur fears comes from his own people. When Harry and Abrasha visit a publishing house with Abrasha's testimony, they overhear a soldier talking about his memoirs. The soldier had visited Auschwitz and Treblinka and proposes to write about them with the help of "two or three refugees from the death camps."[42] Dinur indicates the falseness of such an account from a man who had no struggle with language, such that he continued to "spout like a fountain," and who had been "waiting for quite a while for an excuse to write a book."[43] Not merely were genuine testimonies such as Abrasha's ignored, but false ones appeared in their place. At this point Harry hastily leaves the publishers in disgust.

The Translation and Connections of Memory

The connections which Dinur makes between memories of the Auschwitz planet and this world form the basis of the resurrection of his characters from the living death of the survivor. There are, however, false as well as true connections. The false ones link memories with things of this world which lie about the true nature of the things of the Auschwitz world.

The most striking example of this is the *Star Eternal*'s prose poem "Wiedergutmachung," in which Dinur negates any connection between what was lost in the Holocaust and "making good again" by financial payments. Unlike the true connections, money and burnt families have no intrinsic link. In the poem the authorial voice recalls his dead family, largely with the help of synecdoches: his mother, the "most beautiful of all the mothers in the world,"[44] his father, whose "step was always straight,"[45] his sister with her golden hair and eyes "blue like sky,"[46] and his little brother Moni's childhood games. Against these precious memories he challenges the notion that reparation payments could ever compensate him for their loss:

> I still can't figure out how many German marks a burnt mother comes to. . . . How can I take money for my sister the "Field Whore" from you—and not be a pimp.[47]

For Dinur, the German attempts to "make good again" is a lie, because he can find no connection between what has been lost, and money. The only meaningful repayment would be to restore to him those tiny fragments which remain of the loved ones:

> Give me—
> Give me back one single hair of my sister's golden curls;
> Give me back one shoe of my father's;
> A broken wheel from my little brother's skates;
> And a mote of dust that on my mother rested.[48]

However, there are also true connections to be made between

the Auschwitz planet and this one, for memory not only looks backwards in Dinur's work, but also provides the pathway for Harry Preleshnik, "Phoenix" and survivor, to rise to a new life in the State of Israel. Harry achieves this with the help of his second wife, Galilea, by translating his past memories into his present life in order to discover their meaning.

One method which Dinur employs for this process places him within the Jewish tradition of historical memory. In his study entitled *Zakhor: Jewish History and Jewish Memory,* Yosef Hayim Yerushalmi demonstrates that, traditionally, Jewish historical interest has not been in an empirical collection of historical facts, but rather in the meaning of history. A method which the tradition has employed widely is the categorization of events by the use of archetypes, whereby connections and comparisons are made between chronologically distant historical occurences. The destruction of the Temple became the central archetype for Jewish catastrophe, as Haman was the archetypal oppressor. This compression of history abandons chronology in favor of meaning, as "all ages [are] placed in an ever fluid dialogue with one another."[49]

Dinur employs a wide range of Jewish archetypes in his work. He makes connections between the events he describes and the Flood, the Exodus, Masada, the Garden of Eden, Job, Lamentations, the Akedah, Sodom, Cain, the myth of the Wandering Jew, the Song of Songs, Creation, Samson, the Temple cult, and idolatry. Interestingly, he also uses a number of Christian motifs as archetypes, including the Crucifixion, the Last Supper, the Resurrection, the Second Coming, the stone rolled away, and a monk errant. While many of these are used as metaphors, there is also a conscious process of challenging their ability to render meaningfully the events which the Jews suffered. This is seen in the Dinur's use of the Akedah:

> Were we in Auschwitz the ram? But who was it that was saved from the sacrificial altar?[50]

The Akedah is used here not in its traditional way, as an affirmation of God's saving goodness and the faith of Abraham, but as a question. There is a subversion of the archetype, and in this respect Dinur stands in the long tradition of Jewish writers who, as David Roskies demonstrates in his study *Against The Apocalypse,* use archetypes subversively in order to denote the challenge to standard belief presented by the extremity of the atrocity which they depict. While Dinur continues to employ traditional archetypes metaphorically, they are not used to lend a definitive meaning to the events he describes. In this respect a comparison may be made to the impotence of archetypes in André Schwarz-Bart's *The Last of the Just,* where the interpretative power of the role of Lamedwaf is seen to disintegrate under the pressure of the Holocaust. Like Schwarz-Bart, Dinur emphasizes the novelty of these persecutors, as in this passage from *Sunrise over Hell.* An elderly, distinguished Jew is called forward from the assembled Jewish men of Metropoli, and as he faces the Germans, it dawns on him that

> here he confronted something his forefathers had never imagined: these tormentors were attacking him in his very substance, they were after something altogether different. Now, seeing himself through German eyes, he assumed the shape of an outlandish, terrified, long-bearded fowl.[51]

This passage is reminiscent of one in André Schwarz-Bart's *The Last of the Just,* where Ernie Levy searches his memory for the spiritual resources with which to interpret his sufferings:

> These events concerned someone else. Nothing like them had ever happened to anyone. There was not the slightest allusion to any such phantasmagoria in the Legend of the Just Men. Desperately tense, Ernie searched his memories, hoping to find a clear path, a road to help him through that forest of strange circumstances, which did not seem entirely real though they bore a certain appearance of reality. . . . He found no road.[52]

For Ernie, as for the elderly Jew, the archetypes provided by the personal and collective Jewish memory could no longer be used to interpret his experiences.

Unlike Schwarz-Bart, whose novel ends in the gas chambers, Dinur moves into the world after Auschwitz. Yet as the survivor seeks resurrection and meaning in the new world, the archetypal method is not abandoned; the old archetypes of the collective memory are replaced with new ones from the personal memory. This is central to the search for connections and the translation of memory from categories of the Auschwitz planet into categories of this world.

The formation of new archetypes is seen most clearly in the almost mystical links which join the characters who are closest to Harry Preleshnik. "Over there" Harry's wife is Sanya, who fulfills the roles of friend, lover, and savior. Physically, she is different by having a black beauty spot on her cheek, the mark by which Harry recognizes her dead body in Auschwitz.[53] In Israel, Galilea becomes Harry's wife, but by doing so she takes over an archetypal role defined by Sanya. She even has a black beauty mark on her cheek.[54] Dinur describes Galilea's reading of Harry's testimony, *Salamandra,* as a process in which the two characters merge into one, an encounter in which Sanya hands on to Galilea the task of saving Harry. Similarly, Galilea claims that the mother of her daughter, Daniella, "was burned in Auschwitz."[55]

The archetypal roles afforded to characters are also seen in Harry's murdered sister and brother, Daniella and Moni. Before Daniella is finally "restored" to Harry in his daughter, he "sees" her in other young girls, as if their victimhood is interpreted for Harry by his sister's. In a barn, shortly after liberation, he lies with a nameless young woman:

> His eyes were on her face. He saw her blue eyes, her golden hair. For a moment he imagined it was his sister Daniella lying near him on the straw. Before him now was the face of Daniella as she had been in the ghetto and as he had seen her, later, in the nightmare of Niederwalden.[56]

Later, the girl in the stable and Daniella are linked to another young woman survivor.[57]

Daniella and Moni are restored to Harry through Galilea, who even before meeting Harry has an encounter with the two children she is to "bring back." As she gazes out to sea in Tel Aviv, she sees two young children playing on the beach, whose "little heads were almost touching."[58] Together they were building a "magic" sand castle, which was "growing taller as though it were safe on solid ground."[59] Surely these two children are symbols of Moni and Daniella, whose heads were almost touching in Daniella's locket.[60] Filled with a sense of mission, it is Galilea who pleads to be Harry's partner in a true, constructive revenge, telling him "This is your revenge: your children."[61]

When their daughter is born, Harry gazes upon her:

Cowled in white, peering up at him with stunning suddenness, was the face of his sister Daniella. With the eye of a camera he saw her: diminutive, focused, exact. Just like the day they had parted in Kongressia, Poland, when Harry promised her he wouldn't take long to bring her over to Palestine. The identical blue eyes. As he looked into this face, the Daniella he remembered in the ghetto was wiped from his mind. As if Daniella had never known the ghetto, had never been locked up in the Nazi's House of Dolls. It was as if she had leaped from the moment of their parting at the railroad station, the end of summer 1939, to cling to the folds of the present moment.[62]

The connection which is formed between Daniella the sister and Daniella the daughter demonstrates Dinur's use of new archetypes. For Harry, his daughter is interpreted as his sister, and thus becomes a meaningful expression of his rise to new life in Israel, for it is through the one that he fulfills his promise to the other. This particular use of an archetype of his memory is in keeping with another aspect of Jewish historical memory. For the relationship of a traditional Jew to his or her history is not passive but participatory. In the Passover seder the events of the Exodus are not merely recalled for the sake of reminiscence, but each Jew is called to consider himself or herself as if he or she came out of Egypt. This compression of history provides meaning and identity for the Jew today as it did for Moses' companions. This "making present of the past" in an operative and effective form can be termed "Anamnesis"—a concept which has been adopted by Christian theology as the key understanding of the Eucharistic rite.

The restoration of Daniella can be seen as an anamnesis, in keeping with the self-understanding of traditional Jewish historical memory. Through this device, Harry interprets his daughter with the archetype of his sister, and thus the continuation of his own life, a life which he understood had been "spared to voice the strangled screams of these two children,"[63] is rendered meaningful.

While the anamnesis of Daniella, and the archetypal connections made between characters are a particularly hopeful and striking part of Dinur's work, other connections are also made. Again, Galilea is of central importance in this respect. In his prologue to *House of Love,* Dinur explicitly assigns Galilea the role of the smbol for the land of Israel, longingly waiting for Harry, the symbol of the people, to return to her. When she assumes the role of Harry's savior, she is warned by her father:

"Everyone who comes out of Auschwitz is like a bucket of pus." . . .
And she, without flinching, had said, "Then I'll push my head right
into the bucket and suck it until it's drained." She had sucked the pus
all right. Now he was healthy and Galilea was sick.[64]

Galilea becomes paranoid about the threat which she believes
the Arabs pose to her family, and this terror causes her to eat
obsessively. Galilea's sickness results from her reception of
Harry's Auschwitz memories. As there is no language with which
he can convey their essence, Galilea assumes the role of translator,
both literally by translating his writings into other languages[65] and
symbolically by finding resonances of the Auschwitz experiences
in her own life. Her obsessive eating is a key element in her empa-
thetic internalization of Harry's memories. In her sickness Galilea
considers her husband:

He came to me from the planet of Auschwitz—as if he had fallen
from outer space. He's half-man, half-enigma, and I can't penetrate the
enigma no matter how hard I try to imagine Auschwitz. The only thing
I can understand from his books is the hunger of Auschwitz; all I can
feel is their hunger. Only in this did I manage to get close to Harry.
Not in anything else. Nothing else.[66]

Yet her recovery occurs when she is finally able to face her fear;
for her translation of Harry's memories had, in reality, penetrated
beyond her hunger:

For every phenomenon here she had drawn on a simile from there.
The now that she existed in ran parallel to the plane of Auschwitz, and
her vision of the end here was patterned on the end there.[67]

It is only when she is able to "look reality straight in the eye"[68] that,
with Harry's help, she realizes the connection and confrontation
between the Polish stereotyping of Jews and the Jewish stereotyping of Arabs taking place in her soul. Both are symptoms of the
same underlying human disease, "the suspicion [which] lives beyond borders and climates and [which] is revealed in the eyes of
man."[69] This was the disease that paved the road to Auschwitz.
The problem in Poland was that

[f]or as long as a thousand years Jews had dwelt on the soil of Poland,
and their Polish neighbors never came to know them as one gets to
know a fellow man.[70]

The solution lies in meeting the "other" person in a human dialogue. In the encounter Galilea's vow to prove that "love is mightier than Auschwitz"[71] is finally realized, and not just in a single night of love, which she imagined would achieve her goal.[72] Though it is an enormously costly process, Dinur shows that connections can be made between the memories of Auschwitz and this world. It is therefore possible to talk of the presence of lessons in his work.

The Lessons of the Holocaust

In his work Dinur suggests that the lessons to be learned from the Holocaust fall into the theological and political spheres.

The memory of the Holocaust directly conflicts with the memories (historical or mythical) which form the Jewish religious identity. In contrast to the memories of salvation and liberation conveyed by the archetypal story of the Exodus, the Holocaust has been seen to represent a radical abandonment by the God with whom the Jewish people believe themselves to have a unique, covenantal relationship. Those who would place the Holocaust in the context of God's punishment of the Jewish people for some assumed turning away from the covenant, are faced by a moral dilemma resulting from the extremity of the atrocity—an extremity which seems to surpass the capacity of such a theology to interpret the events meaningfully.

While the offering of a religious response to Auschwitz is not a major concern of Dinur's work, his insights are nevertheless of great interest, particularly in connection with a consideration of memory, as the Jewish religion forms a major part of the collective memory of the Jewish people.

On the whole God appears as an absence in Dinur's work. As young girls are flogged to death in *House of Dolls,*

> [t]he shrieks split the heavens, geyser from the stools out of key, off rhythm, but the lofty heavens obediently keep their silence, as by German command.[73]

He portrays the intense spiritual suffering of Orthodox Jews in the camps through their cries of protest at God's inaction or injustice. On Yom Kippur, Vevke, an Orthodox Jew whose behavior has been exemplary throughout his ordeal in the ghetto and now in Auschwitz, fasts, not in obedience to God, but as a protest:

> "I will show you that even in Auschwitz Vevke the cobbler is equal to fasting on Yom Kippur! But You—You are to sit on Your throne in Truth! Do You hear me? IN TRUTH . . ."
>
> All at once his hands rose clenched at the Auschwitz heaven. "I am a heinous sinner, I am I," he cried. "But what did my Gittel do to You? And my five sons—did they do You some great wrong? Answer! Answer! Why-y-y!"[74]

In *Piepel,* Haiml-Idl's story can be interpreted as a critique of traditional Jewish response to God. This is not to suggest that judgment is passed upon Haiml-Idl himself, for under the extreme conditions he merely uses those spiritual resources which are available to him.

As Haiml-Idl desperately attempts to survive, he interprets each twist of fate which keeps him from the crematorium as a miracle, thus drawing upon the collective Jewish memory of God's saving action in men's lives. He reaches the relative comfort of the Auschwitz kitchen by pleasing his overlords with an impromptu appearance upon the stage of the Auschwitz theatre. There, with the aid of the Musselman cantor Bergson, he sings to save his life. Installed among the vegetables, he asks:

> "Bergson, don't you think that it is the Hand of Providence that put us here?"
>
> Bergson bent down, picked up a turnip, and started slicing. "No," he said caustically, "not the Hand of Providence, but the foot of that Goy sitting there at the window."[75]

Despite his tribulations, Haiml-Idl never quite loses his trust in God. In a desperate attempt to find a function after his ignominious expulsion from the kitchen, he decides to register himself as an engraver. Though he has no idea of its importance at the time, this rash action is to save him. As he stands apart from his condemned fellow camplings, he is astounded by the "miracle" that has saved him, while the others flow like a "yellow river" to the crematorium.[76] Fed and restored for his role, and elated by his sense of having been saved, Haiml-Idl's faith alters his entire perception of the camp. As the camplings line up for inspection, Auschwitz appears to him, not as another planet, but as a place of the normal

world. The barbed wire appears to him like "fishnets hung out to
dry in a fishing village,"[77] and the creatorium smoke "is no longer
the same smoke. Now it is merely smoke coming out of the crematorium chimney."[78] Clearly Haiml-Idl's interpretations of what be-
falls him are based upon his attempt to connect Auschwitz with
the traditional interpretive framework of the remembered world
outside. However, Dinur demonstrates that this interpretation is
fraudulent, for as Haiml-Idl considers the goodness of God's saving
action, he witnesses the death of Moni at the feet of Rudolph
Hoess. There could have hardly been a stronger assertion on the
part of the author that Auschwitz is not a place where God saves
men, but rather a place where a little boy, an "ember of unfulfilled
life"[79] is slowly starved to death and then turned into ashes. How
could Haiml-Idl's theology stand up in the face of this? The theological dilemma which this engenders is similar to that of Primo
Levi's passage about Old Kuhn, an Auschwitz campling who gives
thanks to God when he is temporarily spared, whereas Beppo, a
twenty-year-old boy in the bunk next to him is condemned to die.
Levi calls Old Kuhn's prayer of thanks blasphemous, and what
occurred an "abomination, which no propitiary prayer, no act of
pardon by the guilty, which nothing at all in the power of man, can
ever clean again.[80]

Dinur does not criticize Haiml-Idl, but offers a strong critique
of the spiritual heritage which he draws upon. In his work, this
distinction between criticism of person and of teachings extends
to his portrayal of the Jewish religious leaders, so that he is able
to honor the memory of these great men while disagreeing with
their teachings. In *Piepel* and *Star Eternal,* the rabbi of Shilev is
presented as a saintly man of great personal integrity and compas-
sion, despite his opposition to those who seek an armed uprising.[81]
He is one of the very few who can detect the presence of God in
Auschwitz,[82] and find a meaning in the sufferings of the Jews. He
interprets the present abominations as the birth pangs of the new
nation of Israel—an interesting deviation from the Orthodox belief
that the Messiah would precede that revival. Here the nation itself
appears as messianic. He voices his belief to Ferber, a young Zionist, in the isolation block while awaiting death:

> Can't you see, Ferber, God's spirit hovering here above this destruction
> and Creation? Can't you feel that Jacob—in our bones—now wrestles

with the angel? We are the sinew of his thigh-bone in this struggle! Be strong, my son, at this moment you must be strong . . . from the very blackness of this night Jacob will bring forth the name 'Israel'. Before that, the morning star will not rise.[83]

Despite the deep respect which he shows toward religious leaders such as the rabbi of Shilev, Dinur clearly believes that Diaspora Judaism's traditional advocacy of pacifism in the face of persecution was disastrously mistaken. Here memory plays an important role in challenging the preconceptions that lend weight to the traditional response.

Dinur's understanding of the rabbinic position on armed resistance is explained by Rabbi Sender Frumkin to the would-be Warsaw ghetto fighters:

In accordance with the law of Israel, no Jew is obliged to sanctify the Name except if he is forced into idolatry; otherwise he would be taking his own life, may the Lord forgive me, which is murder.[84]

The definition of *kiddush ha-Shem* given by the rabbi raises some problems. First, the rabbi is concerned with the uprising as an act of suicide, rather than with the moral implications of Jewish fighters killing their persecutors. While this allows Dinur to offer a response advocating resistance, a response within the orbit of Jewish teaching, it is a strange omission. Second, the definition is incomplete, for according to rabbinic authorities, a Jew must not only choose death before committing idolatry, but, according to the terms of *kiddush ha-Shem,* before committing adultery or murder as well. Furthermore, death should be chosen before transgressing any commandment if it is done to demonstrate apostasy, and is witnessed by ten or more other Jews. To add to this, in times of religious persecution, a Jew is called upon to accept death rather than violate any commandment, even if he is on his own.[85]

Dinur focuses upon idolatry in order to challenge the traditional teaching as the true interpretation of the law. Unlike the rabbi, who does not interpret compliance with the German persecutors as idolatry, Dinur uses this metaphor consistently in his work:

That day the Jews removed their wedding rings; their women divested themselves of their gold earrings and family heirlooms, and brought them as a first votive offering to the new idolatry.[86]

The argument is made explicit in Sanya's challenge to Rabbi Sender Frumkin when she calls for an armed uprising, saying:

> We are idolators each time we run, like rats, to hide in our holes and see our children led off to be burnt as sacrifices to Moloch! Idolators, an understatement. We're worse—profaners, blasphemers of the name of Israel![87]

It is not defiance that is being advocated, but a reinterpretation of Jewish law. As the unprecedented Nazi atrocity is set against the old interpretations, a new teaching is formulated—a hard lesson of forceful resistance—as essential to the dignity of the Jewish people. Dinur emphasizes this by witnessing in his account of the Warsaw ghetto uprising in *Sunrise over Hell* that the Germans only respected those Jews who defiantly resisted them. As the Germans proceed with their brutalization of the men of Metropoli, they decide to play a game. "Who is Hitler?" they ask their selected victims. Two men attempt to appease them and are mutilated and murdered, but when a third bravely defies them, he is merely shot; they "did not toy with this third Jew's appearance, did not laugh, did not torture him."[88]

It is this spirit of defiance in the face of persecution which Dinur advocates as the only way for Jews after the Holocaust. In the instances where Jews do take up arms in the novels, Dinur is clearly proud of their courage and tenacity. He gleefully relates how, when the Germans march into the Warsaw ghetto to carry out the final liquidation, their swaggering confidence was destroyed with the first volleys from the ghetto fighters, and the "baby-killing heroes cringed against the walls."[89] Similarly, he emphasizes the bravery of the Jewish fighters by recording the surprise of Polish onlookers:

> They hadn't seen such fighting when the Polish army was defending Warsaw back in 1939, nothing like this.[90]

There is a feeling of resentment in Dinur's work concerning criticisms by Israeli Jews that their brothers and sisters went passively to their deaths. In *House of Love* Harry Preleshnik reflects upon the connections between the citizens of Tel Aviv being taken to assembly points under British escort, and the apparently similar journeys undergone by Diaspora Jewry:

All these people here in Tel Aviv, herded at gun point to the assembly point—how did they dare to malign their European brothers with questions like: "Why did you ghetto Jews go so submissively to the assembly point? Why didn't you resist? Crawl into the freight cars like worms?"[91]

Dinur's theological reinterpretation is linked in his novels to the advocacy of a position very similar to that conveyed by the famous "command of Auschwitz" enunciated by the philosopher Emil Fackenheim:

Jews are forbidden to hand Hitler posthumous victories. They are commanded to survive as Jews, lest the Jewish people perish. They are commanded to remember the victims of Auschwitz lest their memory perish. They are forbidden to despair of man and his world, and to escape into cynicism or otherworldliness, lest they cooperate in delivering the world over to the forces of Auschwitz. Finally, they are forbidden to despair of the God of Israel, lest Judaism perish.[92]

Dinur is more of a humanist than Fackenheim, yet like the philosopher he assigns Israel a central role in his response to the Holocaust. In the closing pages of *House of Love,* Galilea, Harry Preleshnik's wife and Dinur's symbol of the land of Israel, sums up the thinking which unfolds throughout the novel:

With hatred you can only destroy, not build. Even a powerful army cannot be maintained on hatred, only on love—love of country, or love of your own life and the lives of the children you left back home when you went to the battlefield. . . . [O]ur striking power all the way back to the War of Independence has not stemmed from hatred for the Arabs but from love of our land . . . a country has a soul too, and we must act in such a way that the country will love us as well.[93]

In *House of Love,* the connections which Galilea makes between the Auschwitz fear and the fear of the Arabs enable her to work toward a future, not by negating and thereby running from the past and its manifestations in the present, but by affirming her country and her people. The solution which both she and Harry pursue lies in personal contacts with the "other," contacts which break down the barriers of hostility. In this way the paralysis of hatred is broken down and a future is forged which does not forget, but which builds on the agonizing memories of the past. It is an edifice which is constantly threatened by the violence of the Israeli political scene. *House of Love* ends with the death of a young Arab girl who was a sight of hope for the future. She is blown up by an Arab road mine as she is driven away from her village to begin her training as a teacher, a training sponsored as a goodwill gesture by American Jews. The last lines of the novel, in which Harry carries her body away from the wreckage, recall the end of *Sunrise over Hell:*

> And now, as it had then, the rising sun flared in the east. But this time the body borne by these arms was lifeless.[94]

A few hours before, Arab and Jew had sung and danced together under Israel's night sky. To Harry, even at the time of fellowship, it had appeared "a seductive night. Momentary and fleeting."[95] Yet the apparent negativity of the ending does not alter the essential message of the novel. Rather, it indicates that memory is not only fragile, but sometimes very deep-rooted. The Jewish memories of the Holocaust and the Arab memories of brutalization by Israeli troops do not pass away in one night, but need time to forge the new memories which can be set against them. At the end of *House of Love,* the processes of healing have only just begun.

Notes

1. Ka-Tzetnik 135633, *House of Love* (London: W. H. Allen, 1971), p. iii.
2. Ka-Tzetnik 135633, *Star Eternal* (London: W. H. Allen, 1972), pp. 118–19.
3. *The Times,* 8 June 1961.
4. For instance, there is no treatment of his work in Lawrence Langer, *The Holocaust and the Literary Imagination;* Alvin Rosenfeld, *A Double Dying;* Edward Alexander, *A Resonance of Dust;* or Sidra Ezrahi Dekoven, *By Words Alone.* There is a brief piece concerning the book of prose poems, *Star Eternal,* in Rubenstein and Roth, *Approaches to Auschwitz.*
5. David Rousset, *A World Apart* (London: Secker & Warburg, 1951), p. 12.
6. *House of Love,* p. 39.
7. *The Times,* 8 June 1961.
8. *House of Love,* p. 60.
9. Sunrise over Hell, p. 158.
10. Ka-Tzetnik 135633, *Piepel* (London: Anthony Blond, 1961), p. 139.
11. Ka-Tzetnik 135633, *Sunrise over Hell* (London: W. H. Allen, 1977), p. 161.
12. *Piepel,* p. 135.
13. *Sunrise over Hell,* p.1 60.
14. *Piepel,* p. 107.
15. *Sunrise over Hell,* p. 175.
16. *Piepel,* p. 217.
17. Ibid., p. 221.

18. See the passage referred to in note 2.
19. *Star Eternal*, p. 119.
20. *Piepel*, p. 115.
21. Ibid., p. 200.
22. *House of Love*, p. 65.
23. Ibid., p. 234.
24. *Star Eternal*, p. 76.
25. Ka-Tzetnik 135633, *House of Dolls* (London: Frederick Muller, 1956), p. 144.
26. *Piepel*, p. 114.
27. *House of Dolls*, p. 134.
28. Ibid.
29. *Sunrise over Hell*, p. 161.
30. *House of Love*, p. 66.
31. *Sunrise over Hell*, p. 187.
32. *House of Love*, p. 89.
33. Ibid., p. 90.
34. Ibid., p. 116.
35. Rubenstein and Roth, *Approaches to Auschwitz* (London: SCM Press, 1987), p. 266.
36. *Sunrise over Hell*, pp. 19–20.
37. *Piepel*, pp. 107, 204–5.
38. Ibid., pp. 164–65.
39. Ibid., pp. 181–82.
40. Ibid., p. 256.
41. Ibid., p. 278
42. *House of Love*, p. 94.
43. Ibid.
44. *Star Eternal*, p. 120.
45. Ibid., p. 124.
46. Ibid., p. 122.
47. Ibid., pp. 121, 126.
48. Ibid., p. 126.
49. Yosef Hayim Yerushalmi, *Zakhor: Jewish History and Jewish Memory* (Seattle & London: University of Washington Press, 1983), p. 18.
50. *House of Love*, p. 92
51. *Sunrise over Hell*, p. 26.
52. André Schwarz-Bart, *The Last of the Just* (London: Penguin Books, 1984), p. 239.
53. *Sunrise over Hell*, p. 204.
54. *House of Love*, p. 130.
55. Ibid., p. 203.
56. Ibid., p. 41.
57. Ibid., p. 156.
58. Ibid., p. 50.
59. Ibid.
60. *House of Dolls*, p. 15.
61. *House of Love*, p. 133.
62. Ibid., p. 185.
63. Ibid., p. 123.
64. Ibid., p. 222.

65. Ibid., p. 221.
66. Ibid., p. 215.
67. Ibid., p. 222.
68. Ibid., p. 231.
69. Ibid., p. 232.
70. Ibid.
71. Ibid., p. 140.
72. Ibid., pp. 235–37.
73. *House of Dolls,* p. 148.
74. *Piepel,* p. 207.
75. Ibid., p. 191.
76. Ibid., p. 263.
77. Ibid., p. 283.
78. Ibid.
79. Ibid.
80. Primo Levi, *If This is a Man* (London: Penguin Books, 1979), p. 185.
81. *Piepel,* p. 172.
82. Ibid., p. 155.
83. *Star Eternal,* pp. 106, 108.
84. *Sunrise over Hell,* p. 193.
85. See *The Encyclopaedia Judaica,* s.v. "Kiddush Ha-Shem."
86. *Sunrise over Hell,* p. 49.
87. Ibid., p. 194.
88. Ibid., p. 27.
89. Ibid., p. 195.
90. Ibid., p. 196.
91. *House of Love,* pp. 101–2.
92. Emil Fackenheim, *God's Presence in History* (New York: Harper Torchbooks, 1972), p. 86.
93. *House of Love,* pp. 253–54.
94. Ibid., p. 268.
95. Ibid., p. 259.

Miriam Akavia: Redeeming the Past

LIVIA BITTON-JACKSON

"Manyushka" Weinfeld was eleven years old when the Nazis marched into her birthplace, Cracow in Poland, and the sunny world of her childhood collapsed. Thirty years later, the author Miriam Akavia was born out of the trauma of that collapse. After three decades of stunned silence the voice of the poet emerged and, bit by bit, the memory of the ordeal took literary form. On the immediate level Miriam Akavia's writing is a response to the survivor's wrenching need "to bear witness." Although she chose the medium of fiction to tell her story of the catastrophe, Akavia's novels and short stories graphically correspond to the events she experienced as a child and a teenager.

In 1940, right after their invasion of Cracow, the Nazis turned the old quarter of the town into a ghetto and there they herded the Jews, among them Manyushka and her family. They were incarcerated in this mass prison until their deportation to death camps in 1943.

* * *

Miriam Akavia's first book, *Neurim Bashalekhet* (Youth in Autumn), is based on an extraordinary interlude during the Cracow ghetto period. It focuses on two children and their harrowing month-long adventure beyond the prison walls, an adventure which culminated in the cruel end of one the children and the lifelong agony of the other.

Manyushka's parents succeeded in equipping their two younger children, Manyushka and her teenage brother Yeshaya (affectionately called Yozho) with false documents and smuggling them out of the ghetto. They hoped they would be able to survive in the distant Polish city of Lvov under the cover of assumed identities as Gentile children. The book is an account of the formerly sheltered adolescent girl's descent into a life of constant terror, overwhelming loneliness, and harsh physical deprivation. The relationship between the two siblings under these inhospitable circumstances is subtly explored through the young girl's perspective, her attachment to her teenage brother and her nagging anxiety for his welfare. The nightmarish venture at survival culminates in her brother's death and the traumatized teen's desperate search for a way to return to her family in the Cracow ghetto.

The stuff of this first autobiographical novel was the literary portent of things to come. It shattered three decades of silence and was not only a harbinger of a rich tapestry of fictionalized memoirs but also established a pattern. Alienation and the dread of abandonment became basic themes of Miriam Akavia's stories. Akavia's adult characters are bewildered and lonely children, secretly nursing the memory of childhood's lost warmth, while the children in her stories possess a core of adult wisdom and maturity in their confrontation with the world. Both are manifestations of the hurting, adolescent Manyushka who had been brutally thrust into an adult role in a lonely encounter with the Holocaust. The little girl in *Neurim Bashalekhet,* like all the little girls in her stories, plays the role imposed upon her with bravery and wisdom far beyond that required of any adult under "normal" circumstances. And with bravery and wisdom far beyond her years, she recognizes that the only possible option for her survival lies in rejoining her family, even within the prison walls of the ghetto where danger looms so large. It is the adult child who takes the decisive step which eventually saves her life.

Miriam Akavia frequently writes for children because she has in effect remained a child, and will perhaps forever remain the child who became an adult before reaching the age of puberty. And yet, her writing is not for children at all. It is for adults: it is addressed to that core of wisdom and faith that the author knows children possess and expects adults to learn.

The brutalization of Cracow's Jews in the ghetto serves as a source for Tadeusz Pankiewicz's *Apteka W Getoie Krakouskim* (Pharmacy in the Cracow ghetto), an astounding eyewitness account by a Polish Gentile who elected to remain within the confines of this Jewish purgatory until its final liquidation. Miriam Akavia translated Pankiewicz's chronicle of horror from Polish to Hebrew.

It was her first direct confrontation with the unbearable burden of memory. In an article in *Al Hamishmar* Akavia reveals that in translating the work she "took advantage of an opportunity . . . to redeem from oblivion the souls so dear to me, to save them from the anonymous fate of the six million." Akavia admits that "[she] had not found the fortitude and faculty necessary for writing about the most dreadful [experience]." The intimate function of translating from her mother tongue to her adopted language, the language of Israel, the recollections of another eyewitness who was not a victim like her but merely a sympathetic observer, served as a safe medium for probing the depths of her own agony. It helped her to recall events too painful to confront without such a buffer. She wrote: "I took advantage of the translation of Pankiewicz' book, and dedicated it to the memory of the little children who were massacred in the ghetto, primarily to the three little ones I as a fourteen-year-old held in my hands on the day the ghetto was liquidated, the ones I desperately attempted to save—and did not succeed."

Referring to these children, and to others who were so dear to her and who too were soon subjected to the same fate, Miriam writes in the April 1990 issue of *Moznayim:* "Their only graves are the ones within me. Among them new life sprouted and ripened. My daughters. In the agony after the Holocaust I was pregnant with life and death—together. Then they separated. I raised my daughters, and I keep them company just as I am. Because I have been left with the dead. Because I continue carrying within me the many graves of my family, as they do not have other graves beside myself."

Once the floodgates of memory opened, Akavia's repressed anguish surged forth in a stream of literary creativity. One work followed another in rapid succession, each revealing a part of the tale of horror, each divulging a segment of the mosaic which makes up the survivor's tortured soul.

In the English version of the short story "Nelly," reprinted in a 1989 issue of *Tikkun* magazine from the collection originally published under the title *HaMeḥir* (The price) in 1978, Akavia recalls the tiers of wooden planks that served as "beds" for the inmates of the death camp where she, her mother and her older sister were taken from the ghetto of Cracow. The recollection serves to reconfirm the author's conviction that, for her, the secret of survival lay in being near her loved ones. The critical significance of this life-saving togetherness is expressed with poignant simplicity: "I was lucky: I was on the middle tier between my mother and my sister. Here, in this spot, where my right side touched my mother's body and my left side my sister's, here was 'my home.' My heart filled with love and gratitude toward my mother and my sister for placing me between them. A small bundle of personal possessions served as a pillow for each of us. Our coats were our blankets. Beyond my mother's right side and my sister's left side, across their bodies, was reality, terrifying, bizarre, insane. But I was not part of it. I was between them."

*   *   *

Awareness of the ominous threat inherent in that "terrifying reality" is another basic theme in Miriam Akavia's writing.

Almost all reviewers of Akavia's works insist that they are stories of survival. In my view, she has yet to confront the "terrifying reality" of the world which lay in ambush beyond the bodies of mother and sister and which awaited her at the end of the ordeal. Her mother was no longer alive when the end came, and her physically debilitated teenage sister could barely sustain her fragile health, let alone provide a buffer between her younger sister and the world that had perpetrated the horrors of the Holocaust. Akavia has yet to come to terms with the brutal reality of survival. Failing to find justification for survival, Miriam Akavia in time has found a reason for "being," and it is this modus vivendi, not survival, which finds echoes in her literary work.

Manyushka, the critically ill adolescent, was liberated by the British from the Bergen-Belsen death camp, together with her sister Lucia, the only other survivor of her family. She was then taken to Sweden in order to receive urgent medical treatment for a galloping lung disease. It is to Lucia that Akavia's first book is dedicated. In the words of the citation, Lucia was the one who "in 1945 helped [her] to be liberated from the claws of death, and in 1975, helped [her] story to be liberated from within."

In Sweden, Manyushka met Hanan, a bright, attractive boy from Hungary/Romania, and the two seventeen-year-olds became inseparable. Together they joined a Youth Aliyah transport and reached Eretz Israel two years before its liberation from the British. A year later they married in Kibbutz Degania, on the shores of the Kinneret.

Although poor physical health continued to plague her, Manyushka, now Miriam, insisted on assuming an equal share in what she calls "rebuilding the Land." It was the beginning of her own rebuilding. Daily, from dawn to dusk, she toiled in the fields alongside Hanan and her peers. Daily, she was near collapse from fatigue; she was undergoing the tentative onset of the painful, liberating process of return. When the War of Independence erupted, Miriam's fragile health did not stand in the way of her enlisting in the Haganah to fight alongside Hanan.

After the establishment of the Jewish state, Miriam and Hanan joined friends in founding a new kibbutz, Naḥsholim, near Zikhron Yaakov. There Miriam realized that the need to care for people was more imperative than the need for care of the land. She learned from the resident physician the rudiments of nursing—bandaging wounds, giving injections—and volunteered to work as a nurse in the clinic of the kibbutz. As the shortage of medical and nursing personnel in the country reached critical proportions, Miriam sought to extend her nursing services beyond the confines of the kibbutz. She enrolled in a professional course in nursing to augment her rudimentary on-the-job training. "Because," she recalled years later, "after the establishment of the State there was a vast influx of new immigrants in need of nursing and nurturing care." And Miriam nursed and nurtured the living, in order to ease the burden of carrying so many graves, among them the graves of little children. She nursed and nurtured the living, in order earn the privilege of being alive.

In finding her raison d'être in rebuilding the land of Israel and nursing fellow survivors back to health, Miriam Akavia was reclaiming the past and laying the foundations for a new future. She was constructing a new reality in the place of the one she was too terrified to face. She was building a new world in the place of the old, opting for *revival* as a focus of her existence, and as a focal theme of her writing.

Nation-building created many more areas where urgent response was required, and Miriam felt called upon to respond without hesitation. In 1957, when a wave of academicians and professionals from Hungary and Poland arrived in Israel, there was a pressing call for workers to help with their absorption. Miriam was among the first volunteers, and soon she was totally submerged in the work. Eventually she rose to an important position of responsibility in the Aliyah Department of the Jewish Agency.

In 1964 Hanan was appointed first secretary and commercial attaché at the Israeli legation in Budapest, Hungary. Miriam, now a mother of two young daughters, joined her husband, and there, in that distant country, was soon submerged in working for her "Land" and for her "People." In addition to her roles as wife and mother, Miriam acted as consular secretary, nurse, and hostess at the legation. The Hungarian capital then served as a transfer point for Jews emigrating from the Soviet Union to Israel. Miriam's home in Budapest became a Jewish spiritual oasis for young Russian Jews during their sojourn of weeks and even months in Hungary while waiting to be processed for transport to Israel.

In 1967, in the wake of the Six Day War, Hungary broke off diplomatic relations with Israel, and the Israeli diplomats were sent home. (The severance of diplomatic relations is hinted at in the title of Akavia's novel, *Galia U'Miklosh: Nituk Yehasim* [Galia and Miklosh: Severance of relations], see below.) Upon her return to Israel, she immediately resumed her nursing career, this time assuming the position of administrator of nursing at Kupat Holim.

Hanan Akavia's next diplomatic appointment again interrupted Miriam's nursing career. He was assigned to Stockholm as first secretary of the Israeli embassy. In Sweden Miriam served as Israel's cultural representative and official hostess. In this capacity she also had a chance to work with young Jewish Holocaust survivors from Poland who had settled in Sweden. In the Akavia home in Stockholm, these victims of displacement found a vestige of their lost childhood, a reencounter with their Jewish identity. With indefatigable missionary zeal Miriam instilled a love of Israel in these young Jews, who otherwise would have been lost to their people. And her efforts bore rich fruit: during those years numerous young Jewish couples originally aiming to make their homes in Sweden opted for *aliyah* and established families in Israel. In their "redemption" as Jews, Miriam Akavia reached the next phase in her own redemption.

*   *   *

It was during this period in 1978 that Akavia's collection of Hebrew short stories, entitled *HaMeḥir* (The price), was published in Israel. The volume also appeared in Sweden, and later, in an expanded edition, in Germany. Each one of the heroes and heroines in these novellas lived through harrowing experiences during the Holocaust and discovered his or her reason for "being" only upon reaching Israel. Building the Land is the only thing that gives meaning to their lives. And yet, they do not sever their ties with the past. They strive to preserve their memories, and thus their identity, as a guarantee against the oblivion of their loved ones.

In order to preserve her loved ones' memory intact, Miriam Akavia went beyond chronicling the event of the Holocaust. She undertook the task of writing a family saga, the beginning of which precedes the onset of World War II by half a century. In *Carmi Sheli* (My own vineyard; a play on the family name Weinfeld), she depicts the history of the Weinfeld family against the backdrop of Jewish life in peacetime Cracow. And yet, each pastoral scene is informed by the tension of the approaching catastrophe.

The Holocaust shattered illusions of identity for the surviving remnant of the European Jewish Diaspora. The post-Holocaust identity crisis, as yet unresolved, is a major theme in Miriam Akavia's novel, *Galia U'Miklosh: Nituk Yeḥasim,* in which two strikingly divergent elements of the post-Holocaust generation come face to face, precipitating the issue. The young diaspora Jew is represented by Miklosh, the Hungarian teenager. The diametrically opposite Israeli sabra is embodied by Galia, a young girl from Tel Aviv.

Central to the novel is the story of Galia and Miklosh's encounter, and the blossoming of youthful first love. Galia had joined her parents on their diplomatic mission to Budapest in the beginning of the 1960s. Miklosh is a local Jewish youth living in an orphanage located in the basement of the building where Galia's family resides. The two meet, and the coalescence of their different worlds compels a confrontation with their own selves. Galia comes face to face with her ambivalence about her Jewish identity. Miklosh's alienation from Jewishness first challenges Galia's self-conceptions, and eventually enables them to mature. Their bond helps them to grow and to reach a resolution of their inner conflicts.

Galia's parents are overwhelmed by the countless chores their mission in a hostile country imposes upon them. Galia and her younger sister Vered, like all the other children in Miriam Akavia's stories, are compelled to cope with their personal problems largely on their own. They seek reassurance and advice from each other, and find comfort in each other's company in the continual process of contending with the world.

The political dimension plays an essential role in informing the lives of the characters. The novel's background is Budapest, the capital of Communist Hungary which, although it has only limited contact with Israel, displays negative attitudes towards the Jewish state. The severance of Hungary's ties with Israel in 1967 also brings about a severance of relations between Galia and Miklosh.

Harputku B'Otobus (Adventure on the bus), a collection of Miriam Akavia's stories for youth, published in 1984, is informed by the theme of revival. Her characters, native-born sabras, are invariably children, grandchildren, or nieces and nephews of survivors of the Holocaust. Their own lives, however, are graphic paradigms of national renaissance. The author chooses to reveal this at the conclusion of one of the stories. She writes: ". . . but the revival is stronger than everything else . . . all these children are part of that revival which happened to the Jewish people here in Israel."

Yet, all these children, like the national renaissance itself, exist under the long shadow of the Holocaust. The light of their revival, and the revival of the Jewish people, is, in Akavia's writing, invariably dimmed by the dark cloud of the past that does not lurk in the background; it is woven into the fabric of the stories. The children's lives are shaped by the memory.

In "Love from Afar", the young Swedish Karyn's maternal grandparents, survivors from Poland, live in Israel. Karyn knows that Israel "is a land that God gave the Jews," but she also knows that "in Sweden not everyone believes in God and she does not know how to relate to this." Jewish/Swedish Karyn is also aware that "Israel is the birthplace of the Jewish people who suffered greatly." Karyn's uncle and aunt, also Holocaust survivors who live in Sweden, visit Israel frequently, because the "visit in Israel makes them happy and gives them strength to continue to live." As young as Karyn is, she finds her relatives' attitude enigmatic, and she "wonders, how can people be satisfied with love from afar."

Karyn herself has nameless yearnings for Israel, the birthplace and homeland of the Jewish people. But she has to cope with dual loyalties. One aspect of her conflict involves her attachment to her own birthplace, Sweden. The other involves her love for her father and his parents "in the North," who are Swedish Gentiles.

In her writing, Miriam Akavia continually challenges the children's insight into their role as segments of the future mosaic patterned on the past. She reaches beyond the survivor's compulsion "to bear witness," to tell the story in order to produce a record of Nazi inhumanity and Jewish pain. In her writing, as in her life commitments, Miriam Akavia has transcended the task of "carrying graves," or erecting monuments to rescue the past from oblivion. She has adapted the monuments as building blocks for the future. In teaching lessons about Jewish identity, she teaches universal lessons about human relationships. In building the "Land of Israel," Miriam Akavia strives to build a world of human understanding.

Bibliography of Miriam Akavia's Works:

BOOKS:

Neurim Bashalekhet (Youth in Autumn). Jerusalem: Yad Vashem, 1975; also published in Dutch, Swedish, German and Polish translation.

HaMehir (The Price). Tel Aviv: Sifriyat HaPoalim, 1978; second and expanded edition, 1991; also published in German and Polish translation.

Galia U'Miklosh: Nituk Yehasim (Galia and Miklosh: Severance of Relations). Tel Aviv: Sifriat HaPoalim, 1982; also published in German and French translation.

Carmi Sheli (My Own Vineyard). Jerusalem/Tel Aviv: Dvir, 1984; also published in Polish and French translations.

Apteka W. Getoie Krakouskim, by Tadeusz Pankiewicz. Translated from Polish by Miriam Akavia as *Bet Mirkahat B'Getto Cracov (Pharmacy in the Cracow Ghetto)*. Jerusalem: Yad VaShem, 1985.

Harpatka B'Otobus (Adventure on the Bus). Short stories for children. Tel Aviv/Jerusalem: Dvir, 1986.

HaDerekh HaAheret: Sipurah shel Kvutza (The Other Way: The Story of a Group). Tel Aviv: Sifre Yediot Aharonot, 1992.

ARTICLES:

"Twice in Sweden." *Moznayim,* April/May 1978.

"Nelly." *Maariv,* October 1978; in Polish translation, *Tygodnik Po Wszechny,* 1988; in English translation, *Tikkun,* May/June 1989.

"Love from Afar." *Davar Le Yeladim,* 1978.

"Mickelby." *Moznayim,* July 1979.

"Encounter in the Alps." *Iton 77,* 1980.

"The Son of the Shtetl." *Iton 77,* 1981.

"I am Older Than My Young Parents." *Iton 77,* 1981.

"In the Land of Yanusz Korczak." a series of ten stories in *Mishmar Le Ye-ladim,* 1981.

"What's in a Name?" *Maariv,* April 1981.

"Profile of Juzcf IIen." *Maariv,* July 1984.

"Margot." in German, reprinted from *HaMehir,* in *Ariel,* 1985.

"Die Erinnerung an den Holocaust in Israel." *Schatten den Vergangenheit,* 1985.

"Two Encounters." *Moznayim,* March/April 1985.

"The Day which is Night." *Yediot Aharonot,* April 1985.

"Pan Tadeusz From Cracow." *Al HaMishmar,* August 1985.

"A Simple Love Story." *Iton 77,* 1987.

"Love at First Hearing: The Figure of Uriel Ofek." *Sifrut Yeladim V'Noar,* January 1988.

"Polish Themes in My Literary Work." *Poland,* 1988.

"Matters." *Literatura na Swiecie,* Warsaw, 1988.

"Fifty Years Ago." *Moznayim,* April 1990.

"Biography of Agnon." *Jewish Calendar,* 1990/1991.

"The Jewish Writers in Poland Today." *Moznayim,* February/March 1991.

"The Wet Drops of Rain." *Atiryon,* July 1991.

"Short Literary News from Israel." *Nowe Ksiazki,* July 1991.

Translations into Polish of works by A. B. Yehoshua, Aharon Megged, and Sh. Y. Agnon, in *Poland,* 1989, 1990, and 1991.

Translations into Hebrew of Polish poems and short stories, in *Maariv,* 1990; *Iton 77,* 1990; and *Tzafon,* 1991.

Aharon Appelfeld's *The Immortal Bartfuss:* The Holocaust, the Body, and Repression

ZILLA JANE GOODMAN

Aharon Appelfeld is a survivor of the Holocaust who, in his own words, has been "inclined" by fate for "some reason," to literature. He tries to speak, as he says, of

> the individual whose mother and father gave him/her a name, to whom they taught their language, gave of their love and bequeathed of their belief. This individual who, because of the many, has been obliterated and become one of the many . . . is the individual whose essence is the core of the literary vision.[1]

It is this individual of whom he feels compelled to speak, for

> . . . at the moment that simple truth is revealed to you, you are no longer free to deal with the grand and the lofty: you learn to inquire modestly about this individual whose soul you would touch or, to be presumptuous about it, whose essence you would reach.

And he adds:

> This individual is a Jew. Willingly or unwillingly he is a Jew.[2]

One of Applefeld's Jews—Bartfuss—is the subject of this article. A Jew, perhaps an individual or maybe one of the many, he is the protagonist in Appelfeld's *The Immortal Bartfuss.*[3] What is he, this human, this "immortal," that all survivors claim him?

Bartfuss. The name is immediately striking. Divide it into its two German constituents and the result is *bart fuss,* "beard foot." Turn the whole thing around, cognizant of Appelfeld's bilingualism (how could one not be, with this construction embedded in a Hebrew text?) and divide the name once again into two, then recombine the parts, aware of vocal assimilation, and you are left with *bar dfuss* as in "son"/"owner"/"bearing" or "outside of" *(bar),* and "the printed" or "the fixed in shape/formed" *(dfuss)*—in another reading, the immortal "non-prototype" (outside the fixed and formed convention).

What do these readings yield? As Bartfuss—hairy foot, beard foot—the name echoes the late eighteenth-century German custom of imposing absurd names on Jews. In this context it is a name redolent of anti-Semitic practice. It is not a name given by a mother and father "in their language," but a name forced by strangers on a mostly helpless population; it is not an act executed in kindness or loving bequest, but in unrequited cruelty. It speaks volumes in presaging other kinds of sadism perpetrated, in much later genera-tions, by the descendants of those same medieval namers on the descendants of the named. And this while the victims still bore the inscription of their earlier persecution.

In this reading the name connotes the historical continuity of progressive anti-Semitic practice. Append the adjective "immor-tal" here and it reverberates in two directions: Bartfuss, the immor-tal Jew (cf. Ahasuerus); or, conversely, a representation of the immortal, not novel, not unique, expression of anti-Semitism. Either way, Bartfuss is taken out of the category of the individual and placed in the realm of the communal and the representational.

If the gestalt is inverted to foreground the Hebrew, and the Ger-man left as backdrop, the communal still pertains in the rendering of *bar* as "son of," "bearing," *dfuss,* a "fixed form" or "prototype." And if *dfuss* is disentangled from its prototypic/formal denotation, what is left is "that which may be printed," that which can be represented, eternally *(The Immortal).* The implication of eter-nality here suggests repetition, even if not of the exact essence, then at least of intent, so that the story is one that repeatedly recurs and may eternally be printed, written, inscribed. And in another reading—"son of," that is "fruit of," "the printed," which is "the text"—literature, and, finally, the author.

If the Aramaic portion of the construction, *bar,* is rerendered, something quite different emerges. If *bar* is taken as "outside of" or "on the outside," the name changes once again and becomes "outside the realm of print or representation," or "beyond the pro-totype"—and thus unable to be contained either in words or within any prehension of the known or represented. *Bar-dfuss* is eternally elusive, evasive, untappable—beyond even the notions of individual and community, or so individual, so unique, that no known idiom can express it.

In this story Bartfuss is called immortal by his comrades in suffering and smuggling because he has taken fifty bullets in his body (p. 62).[4] There is thus a very concrete and particular reason for his immortality, which removes him from the domain of the communal, of *dfuss*. And where does it reside? It is embedded in his very body, the most visible, observable mark of individuality.

We are told—either by way of the narrative voice, or via Bartfuss's deflected, inner monologue—that he is spoken of with awe and is referred to as "immortal" because "They needed legends, too, heroes, splendid deeds. So they could say, 'there were people like that too'" (p. 60). But this is immediately followed by the comment: "In fact they didn't know a thing about Bartfuss" (p. 61). Thus, despite his singularity, despite any actual physical imprint that inscribes him with a uniqueness, Bartfuss's immortality in the tale is stamped on him by the actions or consciousness or needs of others—by their need for heroes. This uniqueness is not his own. It is the property of the many, part of communal consciousness, coerced by the covetousness of heroism.

How far is that heroism actually expressed in the text? Is Bartfuss, undoubtedly a legend, a hero too? Do the perception of others and his own actions coincide? And if so, is that person contained in the narrative? Does he bear expression? Is he prototype or person? And how is he each?

The first sentence of the book reiterates and affirms the title, while the ensuing paragraphs contain much of the thematic kernel of the tale. We are told, in a short three-word phrase comprising the opening statement of the narrative, that "Bartfuss is immortal" (p. 3), but the reason for this "immortality" is only explained much later. At this stage the passage continues as follows:

> In the Second World War he was in one of the smaller of those notorious camps. Now he is fifty, married to a woman he used to call Rosa, with two daughters, one married. He has a ground floor apartment, not very large, with two trees growing at the entrance.
> Every day he rises at the same time, a quarter to five. . . . He drinks a cup of coffee and lights a cigarette right away. The first cigarette makes him feel very good. For a long while he sits next to the window

and absorbs the little tremors of the morning: an old man walks to
synagogue, a truck unloads a crate of milk. These little sights charm
his eyes. At six he rises, gets to his feet, lights a second cigarette, and
to his surprise, discovers some unpleasant scraps of food in the sink.
The old fury rises in him immediately. But he doesn't let the fury take
control of him. The muscles tense sharply in his neck for some reason,
and he nips his anger in the bud. He goes straight to his room.

His room is practically bare. . . . Once Rosa tried to dress up the
walls a little. She even brought in a table and chairs. That was years
ago, when they still talked. Bartfuss cleared them right out, with his
own hands.

Since then the room has stood bereft of any garment. (Pp. 3–4)

The quite extraordinary opening sentence is flanked by some minimal historical data and then followed by a rather pedestrian description of the fictive present, which leads into a detailed and, by
contrast, microscopic depiction of the assuefaction of Bartfuss's
daily activities. Thus the extraordinary receives scant mention,
while the mundane spreads, at great length, across the passages.
The narrative representation at the beginning of the book is emblematic of Bartfuss's existence. Much in the manner of the text,
his life consists of painstakingly observed minor rituals designed
to lessen the repressed but ever-present historical atrocity indelibly
marked, not just on his body, but on his whole being.

As indicated by the title, the book is a story about Bartfuss. He
acts as the axis of the narrative, with his feelings—or, rather, his
abhorrences, sensations, denials and evasions—serving as its core.
But despite his focalizing function, and in consonance with his
psyche, little of an inner world is expressed. Instead, the text constitutes an array of reactions to the world: reactive thoughts, presented in a deflected manner by way of the narrative voice, or
reactive action, which is usually the response to the perceived
demands of others and to the threat their intrusion entails.

Bartfuss is a survivor. He lives in Jaffa in a "not large apartment"
with his wife, and has two daughters (Paula and Bridget). His life
at the outset of the book comprises a perpetual attempt at fending
off ("He nips his anger in the bud"). He fends off the avaricious
advances of his wife ("the woman he used to call Rosa"), who is
greedy to get her hands on the treasure he hugs to himself and
hides in the cellar. This "treasure," which is a focal point in Bartfuss's life, is really not much of a treasure at all. It consists of a

few thousand dollars, some gold and some objects of sentimental value, but Rosa does not know this, and it becomes an instrument of withholding for Bartfuss. Rosa imagines it contains fortunes of unimaginable bounty, and he does not disabuse her of that notion.

Bartfuss also fends off his daughter Paula (whose approaches are also related to the treasure), and he fends off society at large. Like the treasure in the cellar, he hugs himself to himself ("goes straight to his room") whenever the world seems to come too close to him.

But most of all he fends off words, and his life is lived in a silence he has created. He speaks to almost no one except café owners and waiters/waitresses when he orders food and drink (he eats out all the time and does not take nourishment at home); bus drivers (on his night rides to Netanya); and presumably to those with whom he has business dealings when he does his buying and selling. It is not clear what he buys and sells and precisely how he makes a living. In the time after liberation, in his idyllic days on the beach in Italy, he was a smuggler, and it seems his "work" in Israel is a legal continuation of this.

Bridget, Bartfuss's younger daughter, is retarded. She is not much given to language and is totally under her mother's domination, so that she thinks of Bartfuss as "he" and is quite terrified of him. She is the one with whom he feels most affinity, but Rosa has blocked his way to her. She has cut him off from both her daughters and set them against him. But Bartfuss is hardly blameless in the matter. When some lame attempts to establish a relationship with them in their youth failed, he easily gave up the endeavor.

There are only a few things which Bartfuss actively seeks out: the sea and bus rides—and sometimes, though infrequently now, desultory, wordless liaisons with strange women on the beach. He has removed himself from language and chooses instead to immerse himself, whenever possible, in the womb-like sensations of inchoate sound and rocking movement. But although he seeks solace in the prelinguistic, preform world, he avoids the total unconsciousness of deep sleep. He struggles with it perpetually, so that part of him is always awake and aware, always watching for intrusions from the outside, and especially guarding against Rosa and her curiosity.

Near the beginning of the narrative, in chapter 5, Bartfuss's life begins to change. He is seized one day with chest pains and is hospitalized. This event sparks the beginnings of a new process in him and he slowly begins to relate (if it may be called relating) to the world around him. His new "openness" is reinforced when, sitting at a café, he sees a woman from his past. She is Theresa, whom he met on his way to "that little camp known for its horrors" (p. 48). They had spent the night together discussing *The Brothers Karamazov*. She is the only person he remembers from among the sea of faces that passed him that whole year. Seeing her evokes in him memory and the wish to remember and discuss the past. She, however, neither wishes to remember nor discuss anything other than the present, and she claims not to know him. Her attitude has a paradoxical effect on him: as against her refusal to remember, Bartfuss enters memory and "Now he relived that horrible journey to Dorfenziehl as he never lived it before, in detail, with a kind of visionary devotion. Above the great collective suffering, a point of light shone" (p. 54). Theresa redeems memory for him, indeed, redeems him: ". . . momentarily Bartfuss' life dropped anchor, as it were, at that pier—not exactly a splendid pier, but one that aroused many hopes: Theresa" (p. 54).

Bartfuss decides that survivors need to work for the common good, need "generosity" and "mercy." He forms a relationship with a woman called Sylvia, also a survivor. She dies shortly thereafter, but not before she shows him his lack of generosity. Finally, at the end of the tale, Bartfuss gives away bills of money to a woman— Marian—who, like his daughter Bridget, is semiretarded. Marian is also a survivor. In earlier days she was pretty and gave herself to any man in exchange for gifts that helped her survive. The book ends at this point. Bartfuss goes home and we leave him on the brink of the relief he has denied himself all these years: having entered the world of words and released his anal hold on his treasury by giving it to a surrogate Bridget, he is about to fall into a deep sleep.

This book may be seen as a struggle for expression and a con- comitant denial of words and language, a denial of and struggle against history. The denial of history extends from a very personal sphere—Bartfuss's own history—to a wider arena. The broader aspect cannot be evaded, because of Bartfuss's experience of the Holocaust; willy-nilly he is only partly individual—an "accident" of history decrees that. And yet he can only find his way to history by way of the personal. It is Theresa's individuated form that creates for him "the point of light" into which the "orangish spot before his eyes" (p. 48)—a sign of his impending illness—changes. And yet it is only the retrieval of the personal that allows Bartfuss entry into the communal. Note his visits to the "H.M." or "Holocaust Memorial" (p. 76), and his decision after seeing Theresa that "now he would devote himself to the general welfare . . . wholly for the public good" (p. 76).

Thus history, communal and individual, reasserts itself in Bartfuss's consciousness by way of an individual presence in the shape of Theresa's body. Her body (i.e., her presence) operates on him in a manner opposite to the way his body acts on the rest of society. His body, marked as it is by a personal exposure to a communal experience, has become a general symbol of hope immortal: "I expect great things of him" (p. 62), says an observer. His body has become the property of the many and stands as a quasi-individuated expression of the Jewish people—fatally wounded many times, but still alive.

When thinking about the Holocaust, we inevitably think in terms of the many and thus in terms of the abstract or symbolic. We lose sight of the very personal experience of the physical degradation and pain of its victims. Stripped to the bare essentials of survival, all that is left is the body, its sensations and its suffering. This experience brings a person to a regressive state: like the infant, the victim's focus is that of an intensity of bodily consciousness.

When the infant is in this state, it is still prelinguistic and is, as yet, without separate identity, existing in a sea of sameness, not knowing the difference between body/self and other bodies/outside world. In this universe, it experiences movement (most often the mother's movement, frequently a rocking sensation) and inchoate sound. When sound becomes more coherent and is sensed as a mark of difference, the process of identity formation begins. It entails a separation from the mother. When the sounds become words, become language, the sense of separation becomes more acute. This phase has been called the "Law of the Father," because the father, as it were, enters as language to deny the child the all-pervasive harmony of total union with the mother.

Functioning adults cannot regress so far as to reenter the initial

prelinguistic condition. But it is possible that, in being forced to
live with an excess of bodily consciousness, the adult—with early,
albeit unconscious memory of that state—will be thrown back towards it and desire its comforting incoherence. This is the case with
Bartfuss. Although his connection with the sea may be explained in
terms of his personal history (the stay on the beach in Italy), and
similarly the need for the rocking motion of the bus may be associated with the year-long trip to the camp, it is also equally plausible
that these are related to his need to return to a primal oneness.
Those years of being "starved, crushed into freight cars, [where]
one after another feelings were numbed" (p. 48), and all that remained was the proximity of body, charted the course of Bartfuss's
subsequent desire. This may be seen in the type of sexual liaisons
he chooses, which accord with the prelinguistic form of desire.
Note his first dalliance with Rosa:

> He said, "Come," and she got up and followed him. It was the same
> the next day. . . . She didn't even ask his name. . . . They would make
> love for an hour or two. Afterward he would part from her without
> even leaving her a single word. (Pp. 15–16)

He likes her at the beginning because of her silence—"her silence
charmed him" (p. 18). Later, in Israel, his casual sexual interludes
follow the same wordless pattern. Bartfuss's desires seem to strive
towards the prelinguistic wholeness of the infant's world.

But Bartfuss is an adult who cannot achieve this state fully.
And thus, alongside this form of regression, he is fixed in a later
developmental–anal–stage. This is the mechanism by which he
protects himself, as far as possible, from the invasion and intrusion
of a world of which he is all-too-conscious. His anal aspect is
expressed in his withholding behavior: "Over the years he devel-
oped a clipped language of refusal, protective syllables that were
accompanied with a shrug of his left shoulder, all of which said,
'Leave me alone'" (p. 15).

The anal is most evident in the way he nurtures the treasure he
hides. It is noteworthy that he hides it in the dark and damp of the
cellar, underground, as if in the recesses of his consciousness. The
treasure gives his existence meaning:

> Except for his hiding place, to which he gave a lot of thought, and
> except for the treasure, this alien ground would be barren. The treasure

consisted of three gold bars, five thousand dollars, two necklaces, a few gold watches, a few pictures of his mother, his father's passport, and a small photograph, apparently from school, of his sister. These possessions were very dear to him. He devoted most of his pleasant thoughts to them, as if to a beloved woman. (P. 45)

His treasure comprises artifacts from his past. Holding onto them, desiring them, keeping them hidden—all indicate the need to regress, to return to the past and hold it fast.

Bartfuss became fixed in the anal withholding phase in Italy soon after Paula's birth, when she was struck with dysentery and battled with death for a fortnight:

In those feverish days his language began to take shape, a language with no words, a language that was all eavesdropping, alert senses, and impressions. Even then he learned to mute every sensation. But more than that, he stopped thinking. (P. 21)

And the retentive crystallizes when Rosa announces she is pregnant again (p. 22). Birth and death seem to evoke in him the fear and anger of the Holocaust and cause him to regress to earlier developmental stages. It is the second birth—Bridget's—that firmly establishes Bartfuss's regression.

While the text does not describe the bodily experience of the Holocaust itself, the traces of this experience may be observed in the recurring references to the body in Bartfuss's post-Holocaust world. People are usually described in terms of their bodies. The survivors have, for the most part, changed in their physical aspect. Most of the women in the story (as well as some of the men) have become fat. While this condition may be seen as a natural consequence of aging, and as a change wrought by living in a peaceful world, its repeated mention seems to imbue it with particular meaning.

Rosa becomes fat after the birth of her daughters, just when she ends silence and breaks into insistent nagging and demanding speech. Her broadening out is associated with her entry into motherhood and into language; and it is inscribed upon her by the Holocaust, and more specifically by Bartfuss's ongoing, repressed experience of the Holocaust. It is the result of a development of the acquisitive in her that is, in turn, a result of Bartfuss's anal denial of her and her needs. She too becomes somewhat anal and garners her own treasure, withholding her daughters—who become almost exclusively hers—from Bartfuss.

Inasmuch as Rosa becomes the mother of specific children, she ceases to be the inchoate, murmuring representation of an all-encompassing mother who is but an extension of Bartfuss. She becomes a specific mother and a specific voice. It is at this time that Bartfuss recoils from her and even tries to escape her and the children. From now on he finds her repugnant. He shudders at her description of her daughters as "nature girls" (with the sexual implication in the term), and is repelled by her use of cosmetics. She can no longer be desirable to him, and the nameless female, turned mother, turned "whore" (with her cosmetics), becomes for him the ultimate symbol of all he must gird himself against.

Theresa, too, has become fat, and her fat may also be seen as a protective mechanism. When she and Bartfuss met in the transit camp she was thin. She was the one face that stood out on the "long road" to the camp.

> When everything was locked and dark, Theresa's face had broken through. There were many faces there, thin and tortured, but a clean light, tinged with deep blue, covered Theresa's. All night they spoke about *The Brothers Karamazov.* (P. 49)

Then, Theresa stood out in her association with language; now she is fat and does not wish to remember or speak to Bartfuss. Fat, another form of garnering, has replaced her language. But despite her present condition and because of her earlier individuated form, she inspires in an already prepared Bartfuss the wish to remember (his chest pains may be seen as a mark of the opening up of his solar plexus, i.e., his feelings). "I wanted to exchange memories" (p. 57), he replies to her inquiry when she asks what he wants.

After seeing her and after remembering, Bartfuss begins to release the hold of the anal and move away from the early, primitive, psychological structures. He begins to think in terms of abstract qualities. He becomes desirous of altruism and aware of his meanness and withholding: "I should have been more generous. People who went through the Holocaust should be generous" (p. 73). And together with this statement comes the admission that language is unavoidable now, is more than a repressed substratum:

During the past year I've felt an undefinable kind of mental weakness. All these years I've kept myself from talking. In Italy I was consistent and sharp. But in the past year I've been flooded by talk. Words. I don't know why I'm telling you this. I never permitted myself to tell it. For my part I don't like it when people force talk on me. I hate talk. But in the past year it's been flooding me. (P. 73)

It is at this time, too, that he begins to move away from his former refuge, the sea, and makes contact with Sylvia, the woman who provides him refuge and teaches him the meaning of generosity. Sylvia, in contrast to most of the other women in the tale, is "thin, brazen . . . without a trace of softness" (p. 76). She is very much in the realm of language. She graduated from a Hebrew high school, loves Jewish law and modern poetry: "She made Bartfuss feel she had words to draw him out of the mire into which he had sunk" (p. 97).

Sylvia helps him into the world of forms and human culture, and she does this by way of words (p. 97). She echoes his sentiments, telling him he should be more generous (p. 98). Thus it is that a woman who is not inscribed by Bartfuss's dual reactions to the Holocaust—she is not fat and is thus neither formless mother, nor retentive withholder—operates here much in the manner of the "Law of the Father": she brings him back towards the adult world of social relationships and of ethics, and she does this by acting as individuated sound.

Bartfuss finally gives expression to that which Sylvia has taught him, albeit in a somewhat distorted manner. Near the end of the book he partially unburdens himself of his garnered riches when he forces his money on the impoverished Marion. Marion, too, has become fat, and she also does not remember anything.

Bartfuss is finally released from his stasis, finally redeemed from the tyranny of his body, finally accorded his secret hope: "Secretly he hoped the days would have action in store for him, sacrifice, some plunge that would purify his body" (p. 22). At the end of the tale, when Bartfuss releases his hold on the body and its psychic memories and allows them to enter language and concept, he undergoes a process of individuation and enters into the world of adulthood. It is just when he abandons his will which was formerly focused entirely on withholding, repressing, and protecting the self and its material possessions in a shell of exclusiveness, and as a result enters into the oblivion of deep sleep, that he truly becomes individual. Bartfuss can now become free of the immortality imposed on him by the communal will. He can enter the forgetfulness first of sleep, and then of death.

Notes

1. Aharon Appelfeld, *Mas'ot beGuf Rishon (Essays in the First Person),* (Jerusalem: HaSifriya HaTzionit, 1979), p. 90. The translations of this text are mine (Z. G.).

2. Ibid.

3. Aharon Appelfeld, *The Immortal Bartfuss,* trans. Jeffrey M. Green (New York: Weidenfeld & Nicholson, 1988).

4. All page numbers refer to the 1988 edition.

Aharon Appelfeld's *For Every Sin:* The Jewish Legacy after the Holocaust

AVRAHAM BALABAN

The affinity of Appelfeld's protagonists with their Jewish legacy is a central element of his fiction. This issue was conveyed time and again in his first books of short stories and has become a pivotal aspect of his subsequent novellas. The response of the protagonists to their Jewishness is employed by Appelfeld as a major criterion of their character. Moreover, protagonists who turn their backs on Jewish tradition most frequently meet destruction and loss. However, those who try to rediscover their Jewish roots or strengthen them must grapple with complicated issues of identity. The answers are never simple, but the very search carries a promise.

Appelfeld himself was confronted with his Jewishness in the most traumatic way. Born in Czernovitz, Bukovina to a wealthy Jewish family, he had a happy, seemingly cloudless, childhood. "I had everything a child can dream of," he said in a recent interview.[1] But those happy, carefree days were ended abruptly. In the summer of 1941 he and his parents were staying in a village with his grand-mother. Appelfeld, then eight years old, was spending the Saturday in a closed room, ill with mumps. The pastoral atmosphere of the village was suddenly shattered by gunfire—his mother and grand-mother were killed on the spot. The Nazis, guided by Romanian collaborators, were determined to leave the village empty of its Jews. Appelfeld and his father each escaped separately and found one another later on, at night, in a nearby corn field.

This confrontation with his Jewish identity caught Appelfeld completely unprepared. His mother-tongue was German and, as in many assimilated families, his parents considered themselves part of the general population sharing the Austro-German culture. Actually, during the first years of the war they waited for the Germans to save them from the "barbaric" Russians, he said in the afore-mentioned interview. In his illuminating essay, "Testimony," he wrote:

> Our grandfathers were still observant Jews, but they could not hand down faith. Their sadness, if I sensed it properly, was not that of old age but that of a defeated people. No more discussions, arguments and counter-arguments, but a sorrowful resignation. There were also some angry grandfathers, but they aroused in us only the sentiment every half-assimilated person feels—hostility toward his legacy. Thus, it was an assimilation of a second generation that was taken for granted. No one already bothered to justify or negate it.[2]

Then, without any warning, Appelfeld's Jewishness was imposed on him like an unwelcome yoke. During the years of the war, and later, after arriving in Israel in 1946, he was constantly impelled to examine the meaning of his own Jewishness and the significance of his belonging to the Jewish people. The traumatic encounter between the complacent assimilated existence of his childhood and the "Jewish fate" became a central element is his subsequent prose.

Appelfeld's novella *For Every Sin* must be read within this con-text.[3] The issue of belonging to the Jewish people or severing ties with it is the animated question of the work. All of the textual elements—the different features of the protagonist, the plot, and the structure of the novel—are dictated by this topic.

For Every Sin marks a simultaneous continuation and develop-ment of two tendencies discernible in the author's work over the past two decades. Appelfeld started his literary career as a short-story writer. His first five books, written in the 1960s, were all collections of short stories. Only in the early 1970s did he start writing novellas. Concurrently, the focus of the works changed. The novellas do not portray a single protagonist, as in the stories, but usually delineate a whole group, thus reflecting more general societal and cultural processes. The novella *Badenheim, 1939* is a typical example.

For Every Sin merges these two trends. On the one hand, the novella depicts several groups of refugees in the first months after their liberation from the camps. Appelfeld convincingly describes the masses of refugees, their confusion and lack of orientation, following the end of their long struggle to survive. On the other hand, all the refugees the protagonist meets on his way home turn out to be implicit projections of his own personality, reflecting his own yearnings, fears and vacillations.

This device demonstrates Appelfeld's debt to Kafka. In his aforementioned "Testimony," Appelfeld explains the redeeming role Kafka's fiction played in his life. His first attempts to convey his experience as a survivor were excruciatingly frustrating. Ordinary vocabulary and common literary conventions turned out to be completely unsatisfying. His assistance came from an unexpected place, from Kafka's *The Trial:* "Kafka brought the words back to us. Without him I doubt if we could have raised from the recesses even one word. For us he was not just a teacher but a redeemer." Appelfeld mainly mentions thematic aspects of Kafka's prose, but there is no doubt that he has learned from him the typical Kafka-esque device in which the different encounters of the protagonist are but mirror reflections of him.[4]

Thus, Appelfeld's fiction merges two great European traditions. Whereas Kafka's expressionism shapes the plot and the figure of the main character, Appelfeld's descriptions of external reality, especially atmosphere-oriented images (lights and shadows, etc.) are typically impressionistic. In this sense Appelfeld's prose is a unique phenomenon in modern Hebrew prose. His literary context is not the forefathers of modern Hebrew fiction (Brenner, Agnon, and others), but European schools that shaped the cultural climate of his childhood. This phenomenon is closely related to the fact that from the very beginning of his literary career Appelfeld did not try to become part of mainstream Israeli fiction. He has made the Holocaust, its background and aftermath, his sole focus, examining as well its spiritual implications and commitments. He has never chosen an Israeli-born Jew as his protagonist, and he deals with modern Israel only as long as it plays a role in the life of his protagonists-survivors.

The Journey Home

Theo, the major figure in *For Every Sin,* decides immediately after his liberation to walk back to his hometown, Baden-bei-Wien, a famous Austrian resort town. He estimates that in two months

he will be able to walk the five hundred miles that separate him
from home. Leaving behind his campmates who had helped him
in the struggle to survive, he sets out alone for home. Appelfeld
persuasively depicts the passivity and the lack of orientation of the
liberated refugees. Their old world has been irreparably ruined.
Knowing that none of their beloved ones remain, they are afraid
to return to their hometowns. All their efforts had been channeled
during the war towards survival, and now they are at a loss concerning their future. They passively wait, then permit themselves
to eat the abandoned supplies they find on their way.

Theo abhors this inert behavior. He had worked for two-and-a-
half years in a labor camp, and now he wants to be by himself, far
from the groups of refugees, far from the noises, the horror stories.
He can no longer stand the humiliation of being a refugee. Moreover, later in the novella it becomes clear that he detests the Jews
and their values:

> He spoke of the need to live a full and proud life. A person who doesn't
> live a full and proud life is like an insect. The Jews had never taught
> their children how to live, to struggle, to demand their due; in time of
> need, to unsheathe the sword and stand face to face against evil.

Theo feels that the Yiddish of the camps had corrupted his good
German, and he wants to go back home, to his refined Viennese
German, to his mother, to the world he had known before the war.

His decision implies, among other things, that the Holocaust
was but a mishap, a momentary deviation from the correct scheme
of things. Now one has to restore his old world, and the sooner
the better. Thus, the novella opens with his decisive resolution:
"When the war ended Theo resolved that he would make his way
back home alone, in a straight line, without twists or turns." The
entire book explores the experiential, moral, and social facets of
this decision.

The plot of the novella is minimal, revolving around Theo's attempts to go directly to his hometown and to circumvent the obsta-
cles, real or imagined, that frustrate his efforts. Theo's resolution,
ostensibly feasible and self-explanatory, is rapidly frustrated. Fatigue and hesitations hinder his steps. Furthermore, the post-war
Europe turns out to be a Kafkaesque world, in which walking in a

straight line leads back to the very point of departure, and in which one cannot leave the refugees behind since they appear time and again out of nowhere. Not by chance, Theo mentions on several occasions that his journey takes place "as if in a dream."

The first chapter of *For Every Sin* sets the pace of the novella and its major themes. Theo takes pains to distance himself as much as possible from the refugees, but a rainstorm forces him to take shelter in a tent with some other survivors. He tells them about his goal, and realizes that they themselves do not have any clear plans, other than the desperate resolution to stay together. He hurries out into the rain, wishing to "shake off that contact and the words that had stuck in him." The next day he finds a deserted cabin that had served the Germans for watching and guarding the labor camp. He is impressed by the cabin's "admirable order," takes off his tattered apparel, puts on the German clothes, and decides to stay in the cabin until "[he] uproot[s] all [his] weaknesses and fears." Theo's journey home, then, implies not only severing himself from the masses of refugees, but turning his back on everything they represent. Indeed, it later transpires that he intends to convert to Christianity upon arriving home.

Theo reprimands the refugees for their idle passivity, but he himself stays idly in the cabin for several days, sleeping and wandering around. When he is approached eventually by Mina, another survivor, he rudely protects his privacy. Yet, finally he assists her as much as he can, and even goes on a long trip in order to bring fresh vegetables that Mina needs for her recovery. The encounter between the two is one of the most telling scenes of the novella. Beneath the thick layers of suspicion and rudeness, stemming from the affliction of the years of the war, Theo and Mina reveal the old vocabulary, the old tone of voice, and the old manners and gestures. The confrontation between these two worlds, poles apart, is masterfully portrayed.

Mina exemplifies one of the main devices of the novella. On the one hand she is a refugee, and Appelfeld's descriptions of her fit in with his portrayal of many other refugees that Theo encounters on his way home. On the other hand, she serves as an analogue of Theo. Like him, she had set out by herself, leaving behind the other women in her shed, and like him she falls prey to feelings of guilt. Moreover, though at first he cannot pinpoint whom she reminds him of, he later realizes that she bears some of "his mother's beautiful features."

Thus, the novella progresses on two parallel axes. The author illuminates a nightmarish world of refugees who wander about aimlessly after their liberation, clinging to the mugs of coffee, the biscuits, and the sardines they have found, and to their only legacy of the war: staying together. Yet, this reality serves as a mirror of the protagonist himself. Every refugee Theo comes across is an implicit projection of the protagonist's feelings and features. Some of them remind him of his parents and relatives, triggering an inner journey to his childhood and youth. The journey home turns out to be an internal journey. At the same time it becomes clear that his frustrated attempts to escape from the refugees are an attempt to escape from himself, from those facets of his existence that he detests.

Theo's parents play a major role in this inner journey. In his recollections the mother is depicted as an unbalanced woman who was always ill at ease at home. Only endless, aimless journeys, in which she revered roadside chapels and church music, calmed her down. Finally, after exhausting the family wealth, she had to be hospitalized in a sanatorium, where she stayed off and on during the years prior to the war. Theo, whom she used to take on her senseless trips, conjures up her memory with admiration and yearnings. It is her memory that attracts Theo toward his home, and in order to fulfill her unspoken wish he is even willing to convert. To his amazed Jewish listener he explains that the Christian music his mother adored preserved his sanity "in the darkest of times": "Bach's cantatas saved me from death. That was my nourishment for two-and-a-half years." Yet, the more Theo thinks of her, the more palpable her mental illness becomes. At the same time he gradually extricates himself from her favorite obsessions—music and German.

The father represents a diametrically opposed personality. Collected, balanced, he tries in vain to provide for his careless wife and to keep his son away from her detrimental influence. Unable to pay for her endless expenses, and realizing that she will not change her ways, he insists on divorcing her, despite the pending war. During the first weeks following his liberation, Theo, who never forgave his father for the divorce, thinks mainly about his mother. Still, part of his inner journey is his reconciliation with his father and his values. This reconciliation is manifest towards the end of the novella through his meeting with a refugee who resembles Theo's father:

> Meanwhile the stranger metamorphosed into his father. The way he leaned on the package, the hands, the stooping back that indicated the acceptance of the yoke and resignation. He had become so like his father, that it seemed to Theo that he was about to get up and put on his coat and go out for his day's work in the bookstore.

The stranger goes to Budapest in order to learn from his forefathers how to pray. As in previous works of Appelfeld, music is discovered as the intoxicating, deceptive fruit of the Christian world. The stranger was a violinist before the war: he makes up his mind to give up music, among other reasons, because his camp "was full of music. The commander of the camp was mad about Mozart." That night in a dream Theo sees his father very clearly, and even when he wakes, "the vision of his father didn't fade."

Coming to terms with his father marks a crucial change in Theo's world. The world of his mother, a world of attractive beauty, of Bach's music and refined German, an existence devoid of yokes and commitments, is replaced by the less attractive values of his father. Following this transformation, Theo gives up his resolution to go home. He renounces German and reconciles himself with the Yiddish he had learned in the camp. The verisimilitude of the novella stems from the fact that this change is gradual, almost unnoticed, and even at the end it is far from being final. In the last scene of the novella, Theo is asked by a representative of a small group of refugees to stay with them in order to help to bring one of them to a safe place. Theo still has not given up his dream of returning home, and he takes this request as a tormenting attack. Actually he never decides to stay with that group but simply collapses among them:

> Theo gulped down mug after mug. The hot liquid seeped into him and filled him with warmth. Fatigue and helplessness assailed him. He placed his head on a bundle, curled up as if after a big quarrel, closed his eyes, and collapsed.

Thus Theo's quarrel with himself and with his people ends not with a cathartic cataclysm, but rather with a silent surrender.

The plot which has started with the journey home concludes with the protagonist's clearer recognition that his sought-after home was not a sound home in the first place and that it has been lost for ever. His home from now on will be the group of the humiliated, despised refugees. Opting for the group, the mutual commitments, the Yiddish language, and the Jewish faith, Theo turns his back to his individual journey, to the Viennese German and Bach's cantatas. Finally he understands that the Holocaust was not an accidental mishap in history that can be set right, but rather a far-reaching phenomenon that forces him to reexamine his moral, societal, and spiritual commitments and will affect the rest of his life.

The protagonist's final decision explicates, among other things, the novella's title. The title alludes to the biblical proverb, "Hatred stirreth up strife: but love covereth all sins" (Prov. 10:12). Indeed, the meaning of love is one of the hidden meanings of *For Every Sin*. Toward the end of the novella Theo dreams that he stands trial for his hostile attitude towards the refugees. At the trial he is told that "anyone who was in the camps deserves a lot of love. Without love, there can be no existence. We must be together. Together all the time." Love in this context means staying with the refugees and giving them every needed assistance.

The dream paves the way to Theo's recollection of his bunkmate, Mendel Dorf, who "loved people with a submissive, annoying love, a love full of self-abnegation." Dorf maintained that behavior even in the most difficult situations, until "one of the prisoners called to him, 'Your behavior is a disgrace. For shame! That isn't Jewish behavior. It's Christian behavior, false behavior.'" Shortly thereafter, a woman who lives with the refugees shares her experience with Theo: "I love every one of them. I learned to love them. It was hard for me to love them. But now they are dear to me. I can sit for hours and listen to everything that happens to them." The fact that Theo finally stays with the refugees implies that he has learned Mendel Dorf's lesson, that he has chosen the yoke of love, the burden of staying with the group, caring for its members, ugly and miserable as they are.

Opting for love is essentially connected to the religious aspect of the novella. This aspect, hinted at by the protagonist's name, Theo, has an ever-growing importance in Appelfeld's writings. As mentioned, Theo was brought up in an assimilated family, and he confesses to his fellow refugees that he feels no connection at all to the Jewish faith, "It's distant and strange to me." He intends to convert to Christianity, feeling that this was his mother's wish and that "the place where Bach dwells is like a temple." Yet, during his journey home he himself ascribes religiousness to people whose main goal is to serve and help others. Of the two alternatives, an individual redemption or acceptance of the burden of love and mutual commitment by staying with the refugees, he finally chooses the latter.

Love, the "Christian behavior," is implicitly depicted in the novella as the uttermost human value. Yet, it does not imply converting to Christianity, but rather remaining with the group of refugees, enhancing their chances to survive. Theo does not suddenly become a believer in the existence of God. His religiousness is expressed by the rediscovery of his people and his readiness to sacrifice his own plans for the well-being of his fellow Jews. Some of his companions in the novella try to find their Jewish roots, and it becomes clear that Theo too is about to set out on a journey to reunite with his people's legacy. Appelfeld's theology rarely examines the question of God's existence. Rather, he scrutinizes time and again the experiential, moral, and cultural commitments of the Holocaust survivors to the Jewish people and its ancient roots.

This short description of the novella hints that it is composed as an allegorical morality play. The different characters that the protagonist meets expose his moral quandary and, at the same time, gradually lead to its resolution. The content and the timing of Theo's different encounters pave the way to his final decision and illuminate the importance of his staying within the framework of his people through acts of faith and love. Yet, *For Every Sin* is not a one-dimensional story, since its thematic course is followed by an experiential one, as the author skillfully portrays Theo's inner conflict.

Interestingly, Theo himself is not cognizant of his inner struggle. He is convinced that all he wants is to reach his hometown as soon as possible, but behind his back the author exposes his vacillations and the guilt feelings which engulf him. The various survivors whom Theo comes across gradually establish the thematic focus of the novel, yet simultaneously they force Theo to examine his past and to delve ever more deeply into himself. In other words, the thematic and experiential aspects of the novella are interwoven, justifying and enriching each other.

As mentioned, the whole novella is focused on Theo's affinity with his people. Gentiles are not mentioned at all—only Theo and the refugees. He sets out on his journey home, meets the survivors and talks to them. Once again he distances himself from them and once again he willingly-unwillingly approaches them. The progress of time is described by a few lines: the sun rises and sets, evening lights replace morning lights. In the whole landscape only a few elements are mentioned; hillcrests, empty plains, green valleys. Doubtless, Appelfeld's main concern is Theo's inner journey and not the external reality of the plot. Yet, the few impressionistic descriptions are suggestive, and accurately build the novella's atmosphere: "The cool, transparent lights sprawled on the window-sill and gave it the look of the window at home." Or: "Chunks of darkness, like giant tangled knots, slowly drifted towards the few openings remaining on the horizon. Before long those openings were stopped. Thick darkness filled the plain to its brim."

Typical of his approach, Applefeld does not portray the horrors of the Holocaust directly. Yet the dreadful days of the war are constantly present. A fifteen-year-old girl cannot stand Theo's presence, and her mother explains to him that her daughter is afraid of men. No other explanation is given and the reader can just imagine what the girl had been through in the camps. The down-to-earth tone of voice by which the survivors describe their past and present situations turns out to be a powerful literary device. Appelfeld applies another forceful technique to reflect the nightmare world of the survivors by depicting strange, unexpected kinds of behavior that are received matter of factly by the refugees. The outcome is a world where "normal behavior" does not exist any more, where the line between normalcy and abnormality is totally blurred.

With *For Every Sin* Appelfeld has proven once again that he is a master of the novella. The work forcefully reflects the devastated world of the refugees and simultaneously maps the protagonist's inner world and his attempts to redefine his relation with his people against the background of the Holocaust. The combination of moral and religious issues with personal, experiential processes creates a moving and unsettling work. Although the urgency of the connection with the Jewish people is derived from Theo's specific circumstances, this issue is as relevant and significant today as it was after the war. Through its protagonist's personal story. *For Every Sin* scrutinizes one of the most important problems Jews face in the wake of the Holocaust.

Notes

1. The author talked about his childhood in an interview I had with him in Jerusalem, 8 June 1990. The interview was conducted as a part of my ongoing project that deals with religious yearnings in modern Hebrew fiction.

2. Aharon Appelfeld, *Essays* (in Hebrew) (Jerusalem: Hasifria Hatzionit, 1979).

3. The novella was written in the mid-1980s, and was published in the literary supplement of *Davar* during 1986. English edition, tr. Jeffrey Green (New York: Weidenfeld and Nicolson, 1989).

4. For a discussion of the thematic connection between the two authors, see Hillel Barzel, *The Best in Hebrew Prose: Essays on Modern Hebrew Novelists* (Tel Aviv: Yahdav, 1981), pp. 141–57.

The Reception of Holocaust Testimony in Israeli Literature: Shulamit Hareven's "The Witness" and "Twilight"

RACHEL FELDHAY BRENNER

Saul Friedländer postulates that "the literary renditions of the annihilation of the Jews" express primarily the need "to bear testimony" in order to convey "in a profoundly didactic way . . . some message that cannot be defined but is nonetheless at the very core of their endeavours."[1] In that sense, the survivor's testimonial text intends to engage in an educational process those who did not experience the Holocaust; it contains a message which the reader-outsider is assigned to decode.

Textual decoding is, by definition, a reader's function. However, in terms of both content and intentionality, the survivor's tale presents a particular difficulty; grounded in a historically unprecedented reality, the story resists normative classifications. For the Jewish reader, in particular, the difficulty is augmented since the consciousness of ethnic ties between victim and outsider defies a critically balanced reception while claiming profound emotional involvement.

Hebrew post-Holocaust fiction has reacted to the problematics of Holocaust reception. Especially since the Eichmann trial in 1961, Israeli writers have explored the issue of Israeli attitudes to the Holocaust story of suffering and victimization. Israeli protagonists in such works as *The Brigade* (Hanoch Bartov), *Not of This Time, Not of This Place* (Yehuda Amichai), and *To Remember, To Forget* (Dan Ben Amotz) have been shown entering concentration camps with the liberating armies, returning to the postwar Germany, and fantasizing revenge—all in an attempt to come to terms with the image of the Jew as the helpless Holocaust victim. In other works, such as Shlomo Nitzan's *Among Themselves,* Yosef Bar-Yosef's *The Life and Death of Yonatan Argaman,* and Aharon Megged's "Yad Vashem" (The name), the confrontation of the survivor and the "new" Israeli Jew highlights the repercussions of the tragedy in the social reality of the Jewish state.[2]

A juxtaposition of two stories by Shulamit Hareven, a contemporary Israeli writer, provides an instructive paradigm of Holocaust reception. "The Witness" is a study of denial of the Holocaust testimony. A first-person narrative, it is a story of Yotam, a former youth village educator, and his encounter with Shlomek, a young Holocaust survivor, in 1941. The historical circumstances of the *yishuv*'s struggle for independence combined with the intensifying threat of the approaching German armies contribute to the practically unanimous rebuttal of the victim's testimony of death and suffering. Yotam, like Shlomek, was born in Poland, yet he aspires to pass as a native-born Israeli and refuses to acknowledge the diasporic background that he shares with the victim. Only Ruta, the school's psychologist, warns against the ruthless suppression of the victim's past. The story ends on the note of an irreversible rift between the Israeli and the survivor. Whereas Shlomek severs all ties with the school, Yotam, thirty-five years later, still resents Shlomek's refusal to exchange the identity of a Holocaust victim for the identity of a "new" Israeli.

"Twilight" is a study of identification with the victims of the Holocaust. A first-person narrative, it presents an attempt to enter the Holocaust world. The story draws upon Dante's descent to Hell. The protagonist-narrator tells her previous night's imaginary experience, which took her back to her European birthplace to spend a "one night-long year" with its doomed population. There she watches the nightly deportations, marries one of the victims, has a son and loses him. The tension between the will to live and the desire to die with her people underscores the narrator's imaginary reconstruction of the Holocaust world. Eventually, she emerges from the underworld of darkness and death into the daylight of Jerusalem, her new home. While the voices of her husband and children reaffirm the continuity of life, the intensity of the Holocaust horror recedes.

The stories explore a response to a reality which neither historically, nor geographically, bears upon the Israeli protagonists' personal history. Yet, the first-person narrative in both stories displays the impact of the distant experience of suffering upon the narrators' self-image. The intimate form of an autobiographical account highlights the protagonists' reflexive preoccupation with the Holocaust; the encounter with the victim's reality engenders an emotional crisis which seeks resolution in self-representation. Hence, the "I" narrative signals the depth of the Holocaust's emotional impact: the reception of the victim's story generates the need for ethical self-examination.

Yet, first-person narrative also signals the complexity of the protagonist's self-representation. The limited perspective of the "I" narrator underscores the problematics of a reliable and an unreliable narrator. In Shlomit Rimmon-Kenan's definition,

> [a] reliable narrator is one whose rendering of the story and commentary on it the reader is supposed to take as an authoritative account of the fictional truth. An unreliable narrator, on the other hand, is one whose rendering of the story and/or commentary on it the reader has reasons to suspect.[3]

The issue of reliability takes on central interpretative significance in the stories at hand. Since both narratives focus on the psychological reaction of the Israeli protagonist to the plight of the Holocaust victim, the truthfulness of the account should be sought at the level of the narrator's self-awareness; as a retrospective, the protagonist's account of the encounter with the Holocaust should be measured in terms of his/her expanding self-knowledge. In other words, the degree of the narrator's reliability emerges in his/her conscious self-evaluation vis-à-vis the Holocaust testimony. It is not the Holocaust that informs the theme of the story, but rather the attitudes which the Holocaust has engendered.

Lucy L. Melbourne's discussion of textual levels of first-person narrative offers useful critical tools to determine the reliability of the self-representation of Hareven's protagonist.[4] Drawing upon Roman Ingarden's phenomenological approach to literary texts, Melbourne reads a first-person narrative in terms of "presentative text" and "presented text." While the latter consists of the narrator's utterances which project the narrator himself/herself and the world as he/she perceives it, the former constitutes the "suppressed" narrative in the explicit text.[5] The "frame" of the suppressed text emerges from the narrator's self-presentation and projects the narrator as an object of analytical interpretation. Melbourne submits that

> . . . in first-person fiction—especially in unreliable narration—it is this concept of direct presentation as implicit exhibition which is the literary-critical skeleton key capable of unlocking the self-enclosed test.[6]

Both Rimmon-Kenan and Melbourne, then, predicate the correct decoding of the reliability of the narrator upon the reader's sensitivity to the ironic discrepancy between the obvious intention of the narrator and the latent meaning that such an intention projects. In both "The Witness" and "Twilight," however, the distinction between the roles of first-person narrator and the reader seems to deviate somewhat from the paradigmatic levels of the narrator's explicit story and the reader's discernment of the suppressed content in the presented text. Since these stories represent responses to another story—the story of the Holocaust—the reliability of the narrative is measured in terms of *the narrator*'s consciousness of his/her reception of the Holocaust story. His/her tendency or reluctance to suppress or avoid the story of horror determines the reliability of the narrative. The function of the reader/critic, therefore, does not consist in salvaging the "suppressed text" from the narrator but, rather, in assessing the extent of the narrator's awareness of his/her un/reliability.

In that sense, the effectiveness of the "didactic message" of the Holocaust testimony may be defined in terms of the recipient's ability to examine the nature of his/her response to the victim and his tale. Hareven's stories demonstrate a progression from a limited to an extensive degree of self-awareness. Whereas the narrator in "The Witness" provides an indication of *some* awareness of his contradictory responses in his narrative, the contrived fictional form of the first-person narrative in "Twilight" exhibits a degree of consciousness which practically eliminates the sense of suppressed self-knowledge.

In his phenomenological study of memory, William Earle maintains that recollection "brings to mind what has passed out of it, and by an effort of will. we recall what we wish or need to recall for present purposes."[7] The "present purposes" of Yotam's recollection in "The Witness" become clear only in the final paragraph of the story, which registers the transfer from the recollected past into the present moment of recalling. Switching from the detailed, sequential rendition of his relationship with Shlomek, a relationship which ended in the young boy's failure to communicate his testimony of the Holocaust to the community, Yotam goes on to summarize briefly the events that followed Shlomek's abrupt departure from the youth village. He tells about the publication of Shlomek's testimony, and expresses his anger at Shlomek's inconsiderate behavior, accusing him of being irresponsible and hasty when acting independently to convey his message. The content of the concluding passage does not seem to register any attitudinal change in Yotam's response to the victim and his story. While reluctantly admitting that Shlomek was telling the truth about the atrocities of the Holocaust, Yotam still blames the survivor for his insistence on impressing his truth in a wrong fashion and at a wrong time.[8]

A close reading of the concluding section, however, reveals a fundamental shift which provides an insight into the "present purpose" of the narrative as a whole. At this very late stage in the story, the perspective changes altogether, with the introduction of one who is hearing the narrative. Addressing this listener directly for the first time, Yotam says:

> Don't mind my anger. I always get angry when I recall Shlomek's case, even now, so many years later. I am telling you, he was ungrateful, very ungrateful. Here, look, that year his testimony was published in an important newspaper, two-and-a-half columns long. I keep it in my drawer, of course I keep it, I keep everything, albums, photographs. Boaz in his uniform. A high-ranking officer, of course, a high-ranking officer. A letter to school from Eli . . . [who] was killed later in the Six Day War. A card from Rina from Norway. Yes, it's me with the graduating class. Look at my hair, look . . . So, Shlomek's testimony is also with me, after all I was his tutor, I welcomed him to the country . . . I kept this testimony.[9]

The conclusion of the story introduces a new generic distinction. The presence of a listener signifies that this is an oral account. The dramatics of an oral first-person presentation suggests the narrator's urgent need to re-view the past. At the same time, the anonymous listening agent shifts the narrative focus in that the presenting subject becomes a presented object. Yotam's address to his listener situates him in the role of a defendant, eager to justify himself. The sense of urgency is underscored by the rhetorical discrepancy of rhythm and diction between the narrated story and Yotam's concluding argumentation. The story about Shlomek presents a carefully selected and sequentially ordered recollection, starting with Shlomek's arrival in the youth village and ending with his flight to Jerusalem. Punctuated with Yotam's candid account of his personal life, the narration clearly aims at a reliable and objective rendition of past events. Thus, the conclusion, which features repetitions, fragmentary phrases, a disjointed time frame, and appeals to the listener, undermines the sense of a progressively unfolding recollection; it introduces a notion of inner confusion and uncertainty.

Hence, in terms of the narrator's reliability, the tension between the voice of the narrated past events and that of the concluding passage relating to the present signals emerging consciousness of the suppressed text in the narrative. The abrupt rhetorical breakup indicates the narrator's growing disappointment with his "presented text." The undertone of frustration in the last sentence of Yotam's account of the testimony-related events in the village marks the transition to the final step of his rather incoherent appeal to the listener's sympathy: "There was a sense of heavy blow in Shlomek's affair, and I admit that I could not define it."[10] On the one hand, the statement presents a vivid recollection of guilt experienced thirty-five years before, and the inability (or, perhaps, the unwillingness) to explore its significance at that time. On the other hand, Yotam's present acknowledgment of the sense of unease vis-à-vis the victim, communicates the rationale for relating the story so many years later. The act of telling conveys the persistent sense of guilt and, at the same time, denotes the "present purpose" of the recollection, namely, the desire to resolve this emotional predicament.

The component of the listening agent highlights the narrator's search for sympathetic understanding which would relieve the pervasive sense of failure. Yotam's recurring appeals to his silent listener establish the confessional mode of his account, whereas the need to secure a sympathetic reception of the confession projects the emerging insight into the meaning of the "heavy blow" inflicted by "Shlomek's affair." This insight, however, is never fully articulated. Yotam seems unable to fully acknowledge the extent of his insensivity toward the Holocaust victim; neither is he capable of consciously relinquishing the *yishuv*'s ideology which places social conformity above the individual's well-being. Yet, the restlessness noticeable in both his disjointed narrative as well as in the impulsive production of supporting "exhibits"—the memorabilia relating to his students—manifests the sense of "unfinished business" which propels the need to seek self-justification. The thirty-five-year-old newspaper clipping of Shlomek's testimony that Yotam presents to his listener exemplifies what Melbourne terms the "concept of direct presentation as implicit exhibition" of the suppressed text.

Yotam presents Shlomek's testimony as one of the memento's of his career in education. Ostensibly, the clipping of Shlomek's published testimony is meant to demonstrate Yotam's forgiving magnanimity and generosity of spirit, despite Shlomek's "ingratitude" towards Yotam and the school; he keeps the testimony with objects that demonstrate Yotam's important contribution to the supreme task of raising the generation of new heroic Israelis. Yet, the inclusion of the testimony of a Holocaust victim among the evidence which confirms Yotam's idealization of the "new" Israeli reveals an inconsistency at the very core of his ideological stance. As a story of Jewish suffering and victimization, the testimony undermines the *yishuv*'s position of *shelilat ha-golah* (negation of the Diaspora) to which both Yotam and his students have subscribed. As Yotam recalls, the students Boas, Eli, and Rina—the same students whose pictures, letters, postcards Yotam keeps along with Shlomek's testimony—brutally repudiated Shlomek's story about his murdered family.[11] Yotam also recalls how he himself used to advise Shlomek not to tell his story because it set him apart from his friends; he should try, Yotam would repeatedly tell Shlomek, to be "like everybody else."[12]

In an ironic reversal, the narrator brings forth Shlomek's previously silenced and ignored testimony to sustain the reliability of his own testimony, which he feels compelled to articulate. Thus the testimony, which nobody wanted to hear thirty-five years before and which is now produced as a piece of extenuating evidence in a narrative of self-justification, marks the extent of Holocaust reception. The reemergence of Shlomek's text in the confessor's text signals the unacknowledged but increasingly powerful under-current of affinity with the victim.

In his study *Confession and Complicity in Narrative,* Denis A. Foster postulates that "[s]in can be spoken only in symbols of negation . . . the confessor can only speak of innocence by speaking of sin, reenacting in the language of confession the loss he feels."[13] Foster's discussion of sin in terms of lost innocence illuminates the psychological underpinnings of Yotam's autobiographical text. Yotam preserves the text of the initially denied Holocaust testimony; he also insists on confessing the act of denial. Paradoxically, the victim's tale has remained with the Israeli despite his ostensible desire to obliterate the story. Moreover, the reenactment of the denial signals a lifelong need to relive that segment of the past which focuses on the victim's testimony. The testimony of denial thus emerges as a pivotal event in the life of an Israeli who, so many years later, still protests his innocence.

Yotam's continuing anger at Shlomek's "arrogance," in insisting on asserting his past despite the programmatic, future-oriented platform of the "authoritative national institutions"[14] implies the suppressed text of *his* self-dissatisfaction stemming from *his* reneging on the past in order to conform. Apparently too painful to articulate, the suppressed consciousness of self-betrayal emerges in Yotam's contradictory treatment of the victim's testimonial text. I have already commented on the paradoxical signification of Yotam's decades-long preservation of Shlomek's published story in view of his ideological persuasion. This peculiar attachment to the testimony of Jewish suffering offers an interesting psychological insight when juxtaposed with the circumstances of the initial rejection of Shlomek's text, as recounted in Yotam's recollection.

Ruta and Yotam, who "against his better judgment" informed the psychologist about Shlomek's assiduous nightly writing, look at Shlomek's tightly written pages. Yotam recalls the following conversation:

> "Is it in Polish?" Ruta asked me.
> "Polish," I said. I was displeased to still be able to identify this language and even read it, if I have to. My mother insists on speaking Polish with me and even writes to me in this language, and I cringe. I don't like this language, to say it plainly.
> "O.K. Read then," said Ruta . . .

"I can't," I said, and not the whole truth did I say. "My mastery of this language is limited to very few words."

Rutha looked at me impatiently.

"If so, my friend, I can't help you right now . . ."

She said it and ran to the bus. Had Ruta waited a bit, I may have reconsidered, but Ruta did not wait. She never gave anybody the chance to change his mind . . . I do not blame her. She was a very busy woman, working day and night with our pupils who needed her.[15]

This passage is important on several accounts. At the level of content clarification, it provides the explication of Yotam's sense of remorse which prompts his confession; his commentary on his conduct clearly expresses the guilt and regret over his refusal to read his pupil's story. The lie which precluded his intervention at a crucial moment induces a sense of profound failure as an educator.

At the deeper level of the suppressed text, the denial of the victim's testimony amounts to self-denial. It is of crucial importance that Yotam was born in Poland and, as he reluctantly admits, is still capable of communicating in this language with his mother. Yotam's refusal to read Shlomek's testimony in Polish signifies, therefore, first and foremost the desire to obliterate *his* Diasporic roots. Yotam's rejection of his mother tongue spells out severance with the diasporic heritage that his mother represents. In the context of Yotam's response, the notions of mother and tradition have become synonymous. The preservation of Holocaust testimony thus represents a constant reminder of the narrator's self-betrayal; his lifelong dissatisfaction at the outcome of Shlomek's case originated, in effect, in his deprecatory self-image of a Diaspora-born Jew. Yotam's pretense to pass, at any cost, as a "native" Israeli—the antithesis of the suffering Diaspora victim—delineates, to recall Foster's observation, the sinner's lost innocence which he wishes to regain through confessionary reenactment of his sin, namely, the refusal to relate to his own past through the Holocaust story.

The absence of the complete text of Shlomek's testimony in the story is significant in that it focuses attention on the recipient of the testimony, rather than on the victim. The Holocaust tragedy is only fragmentarily depicted in Shlomek's altercations with the class, and is formulaically presented in his code, which lists the names and the ages of his murdered family members: "Y[father]-39, B[mother]-37, E[brother]-12, Y[brother]-9" (pp. 44, 52). The full testimony which Yotam refuses to read is later published in an "important newspaper" which Yotam keeps, yet never reproduces in his autobiographical account.

Thus the "didactic message," as Friedländer terms it, of the victim's tale emerges at the level of the testimony's reception. In that sense, the testimony becomes a catalyst which initiates the process self-reexamination. Ironically, the refusal to recognize affinity with the victim results in an emotional fixation on the victim's disrupted testimony; the consciousness of the victim's unheard story arouses a sense of anxiety powerful enough to engage the recipient in a confessional narrative. The inability to confront the testimonial text even at the confessional stage demonstrates an ambivalent attitude in terms of the narrator's acknowledgment of his narrative's suppressed text. The resistance to discern the links which tie him to the victim precludes an honest self-confrontation which might lead to inner reconciliation. The reliability of the narrator in terms of Holocaust reception remains limited. Though the first-person narrative in "The Witness" produces a confessional account, the narrator remains unable to consciously assess his fear of identification with the victim's tale—which, but for "a geographic accident,"[16] could have been his own.

In "Twilight," Hareven explores the possibility of full realization of the accidental nature of Jewish existence. The protagonist-narrator in this story responds to the testimony of destruction in terms of identification. Like Yotam, the narrator in "Twilight" left Europe for Israel before the war started. In contrast with Yotam's avoidance of the tragic content of the testimony, however, the first-person narrator in "Twilight" strives to receive the Holocaust story as her own, to relive the victim's fate.

The issue of the narrators' assumed and omitted names marks the contrast between the two narratives in terms of the determination to dissociate from, and the desire to reintegrate into, the lost world of childhood. The narrator of "The Witness" establishes his new identity of "a typical *sabra,* an educator of *sabras*"[17] by changing his name from Rozovsky to Yotam Raz. He fails, however, to notice the ironic denotation of his new name. "Yotam" derives from the Hebrew root *yatom,* which designates an orphan, while the substantive "raz" signifies a secret. Metaphorically, the new name is meant to enhance his organically Israeli identity. Literally, however, the new name reveals Yotam's secret: it spells out his rootlessness. In that sense, the name points to the suppressed text of its bearer's ambivalent sense of identity.

The namelessness of the narrator in "Twilight" signals the impossibility of penetrating the world of the victim. On the one hand, the anonymity of the narrating agent communicates a sense of affinity with the Holocaust victims whose mass death robbed them of their identity. When she watches how "[p]eople in their festive clothes [were] piled up on the trucks, and there was no more telling them apart . . ." she senses an uncontrollable urge to join them, to be like them: "I wanted, wanted mortally . . . to go out to the opera square. Together with all the children. Together with all the neighbors. . . ."[18] On the other hand, her namelessness marks her otherness: a living person, she is a stranger in the land of the dead. The inhabitants of the city never address her by her proper name, though they know her; as for her, she recognizes them and remembers their names.

The narrator's namelessness is significant not only in relation to the victims, but in terms of *her* diasporic roots and identity. Once her imagination allows her to reenter her birthplace, she discovers that she has irrevocably lost her past; the destruction of the city and its population has ruled out the possibility of restoring, even in a dream or fantasy, the sense of her childhood experience. At one point, the man whom she marries leads her into "a vast deserted residence." The mansion, filled with "heavy, very rich furniture, a sideboard and carpets and enormous armchairs, and crystal chandeliers" which belonged to generations of her "forefathers and grandmothers," appears to verify her lifelong expectation that "this house existed behind some wall or other, and that one day [she] would inherit it." This hope, however, never materializes: the narrator and her "husband" decide that they "would use only one of the rooms, a plain and all but empty one. . . ."[19] The mansion is never revisited, nor does the narrator come into her inheritance: in the reality of the Holocaust, the family heirloom, history, and tradition remain out of limits; they recede behind walls.

Thus, her family name, a symbol of generational continuity, has ceased to exist in that it has lost its meaningfulness. Similarly, her proper name, a sign which marks entrance into the world as an individual as well as the metonymic signifying of the uniqueness of her personal history, is omitted in the protagonist's narrative. The empty room becomes filled with wedding gifts which hold "all the toys [she] had lost as a child and never found." The childhood toys, bought at one time for *her,* are, like the residence, shown for a moment and never referred to again. Significantly, the "cases and cartons and beribboned boxes," which she never shifts, hardly leave any space to move in the room in which they "lived like lizards, in crevices, among the empty cases. . . ."[20] Like the family residence which has become unfunctional, the lost toys, the signs of the narrator's childhood past, have become empty objects which render her former self empty of identity, nameless.

As the metaphors of both the residence and the toys seem to indicate, the reality of the Holocaust has rendered meaningless the formative experience of the Diaspora; the destruction has robbed the narrator of her cultural and historical inheritance. Her insistent search for the past brings forth the realization that the traditional frames are void, displaying the nothingness of horror and death; her painful experience of the *recherche du temps perdu* demonstrates that new patterns are required to construct the post-Holocaust world. Indeed, the new content is communicated at the conclusion of the story when the unnamed first-person narrator emerges from her nightmarish fantasy of "the year-long one night" stay in her Diaspora hometown into her Jerusalem home full of sunlight.

In her discussion of post-Holocaust poetry, Sidra Ezrahi refers to "Twilight" to support her thesis that the "lure of the sun and the pull of the earth" in modern Israeli fiction and poetry "facilitate a kind of selective amnesia that serves the regenerating spirit of the community." Ezrahi then contrasts the Israeli approach with that of the writer-survivor who "is resisting the territorial imperative and the centripetal thrust of a collective homecoming."[21] It would appear that, in view of the immense emotional impact of the Holocaust reality in Hareven's stories, such a clear-cut distinction needs further qualification. We have already seen in "The Witness" that the Israeli narrator's predilection for selective amnesia brings to the fore a long-standing emotional dis-ease which seeks relief in confession. Yotam's inability to finalize his self-examination with a conscious recognition of the discrepancy between the "presented text" and the "suppressed text" in his confession, underscores

Hareven's awareness of the psychologically detrimental effect of the response to the Holocaust from the position of the politics of "the territorial imperative."[22]

The narrative in "Twilight" presents an even more complex approach to the Holocaust tale. Whereas "The Witness" focuses on the problematics of conscious acknowledgment of the victim, "Twilight" deals with the problematics of total identification with the victim's fate. While Yotam's confession stems from his guilt at having dissociated himself from the victim, the first-person narrative in "Twilight" explores the guilt for having escaped the fate of the victim. By "returning" to the city of her birth, the narrator in "Twilight" signals the ability to confront a truth which Yotam is unable to recognize, namely, the "accident of geography" which saved her life. Her anonymity as well as the anonymity of her hometown communicate the universality of her predicament. Furthermore, the absence of a listener in the text demonstrates the directness of her approach: no intermediaries between narrator and reader are required, since both are in the same situation: by virtue of an accident of geography or history, both the narrator and her readers are alive and, therefore, share the irrational sense of guilt for being alive.

The resolution of guilt requires reconstruction of the events which led to the inception of guilt. Yotam's confession, for instance, presents a reconstruction of events which culminates with the denial of the victim's testimony. The recollection brings forth the confessor's transgression of self-denial in terms of his past and thus elucidates, for the reader if not for the confessor, the source of guilt. The sense of guilt in "Twilight," however, does not evolve from an experience; it is precisely the absence of a specific experience of suffering that causes the sense of guilt. Paradoxically, therefore, the resolution of the narrator's emotional problem involves a reconstruction of events which *could have been* experienced. Since the Holocaust represents a historically unprecedented catastrophe, the reconstruction of the Holocaust reality by the narrator, who did not experience it, presupposes a fictional situation to help clarify the root of the psychological predicament.

It is of crucial importance that the narrator in "Twilight" presents her story as fiction. In fact, it is the contrived construction of the story that attests to the narrator's reliability; from the beginning, the teller ensures that the story will not be considered a rendition of a factual Holocaust experience. Since the seams of her fictional fantasy are deliberately exposed, the reader has no reason to suspect the reliability of the narrator, to recall Rimmon-Kenan's definition. In other words, the discrepancy between the "presented text" and the "suppressed text," in Melbourne's terms, practically disappears.

The story is told twice: its introduction presents a synopsis that is followed by a detailed account of the imaginary experience. Thus any mistaken notion of authenticity is disclaimed from the outset:

> Last night I spent a year in the city where I was born. I have long known the password for getting there: Dante's line, "I am the way to the city of sorrow." In a clear voice I said, *"Per me si va nella città dolente,"* and time split open and I was there. In that night's year I met a man, married, became pregnant, and gave birth to a child who grew fast, all without light.[23]

This introduction clearly communicates the narrator's desire to see again her birthplace, as well as the realization that such experience may actualize only in her imagination. The evocation of the experience defies the notion of factuality: a night contains a year; distances disappear; a proper password rearranges time. The source of the fantasy is clearly annotated: it is Dante's entrance to Hell.

As the introduction demonstrates, the narrator has consciously searched for an adequate technique to approach the Holocaust world. The analogy between Dante's Hell and the imagined hell of the Holocaust is clearly delineated in the story of the narrator's sojourn in the city. Like Dante, the narrator watches the multitudes of the doomed, is recognized as a living soul among the nonliving, and must dream herself out of the "city of sorrow." The paradigm of Dante's canto 3 worked into the representation of the Holocaust constitutes an acknowledgment of the impossibility of recreating the reality of the Holocaust. The horror of the Holocaust remains beyond language and imagination; it can be approximated only through related intertexts.

In his discussion of inherited and chosen metaphors in Holocaust representations, James Young postulates that "even with the dangers of archetypal thinking . . . apparent, there may be no alternative: to think about, to remember, and to express events is either to do so archetypally and figuratively—or not at all."[24] "Twilight" presents such an attempt to explore the un/reality of the catastrophe in an analogous representation. Whereas the confession in "The Witness" demonstrates the consequences of the long-lasting refusal to recognize the catastrophe, the analogy to Dante's Hell in "Twilight" indicates the intensity of the desire to expiate the sense of guilt by confronting the horror of annihilation.

Since the story, as a rewritten Dantean text, evolves in the narrator's imagination, the importance that she allots to the victim indicates the insistence on decoding the didactic message of the Holocaust testimony. Therefore, the nature of her encounter with the man she marries and has a child with is of particular importance; like Virgil who comes from the dead to lead Dante into the horrifying mystery of Hell, the man she meets at the opera—the grotesque mirror of the Holocaust theatrical un/reality—comes from the Holocaust dead to guide her through the "city of sorrow." He relates to her the "mechanics" of the annihilation. The fantasy of marital attachment to him communicates the willingness to live with the tale of suffering and death.

In her identification with the victim, the narrator pushes further into the realm of sorrow and mourning. In her fantasy of wifehood and motherhood in the world of the Holocaust dead, she is capable of actually feeling the pain of loss:

> Toward the end of the year I gave birth. The child tore away from me at one stroke; and I remembered dimly that once, long ago, in my other life, I had loved a man very much, and it was just this way I had felt when he tore away from my body: as though a part of me had suddenly been separated for all time. Then I wept many tears.[25]

Significantly, the pain of loss is related to the female body. The Holocaust, in its most fundamental sense, amounts to the nullification of motherhood. In the world of murdered children, the functions of conception and birth have been abrogated. In the city where she grew up as a child, the narrator imagines herself as a mother and finds out that both her childhood and her child have been taken away from her. The loss instills the desire to die with the doomed, to "say to all the children: Wait for me. I shall say: I am coming with you, of course I am coming with you."[26]

The way back to the land of light and life leads through an operating room in which the desire to resume the role of wife and mother must be surgically/symbolically reimplanted. The scene of bodily repair that concludes the narrator's nightmare of the descent into the world of the Holocaust dead implies the concreteness of the price that those who remained alive "by accident" must pay to lead normal lives. It also implies that in the mind of the living, the world of the dead cannot coexist with the world of normalcy. It is, therefore, significant that the story concludes with the narrator getting up to make breakfast for her husband and children. This mundane task, totally meaningless in the world of the dead, where food preparation amounts to a theatrical gesture, symbolizes the restored meaningfulness of family life.

Neither of the two stories offers a conclusive answer to the problematics of Holocaust reception in the reality of Israel. On the one hand, the nightmarish experience of the narrator in "Twilight" helps one understand, though not condone, the cowardly behavior of the narrator in "The Witness." On the other hand, Yotam's life-long frustration and self-dissatisfaction illuminates the significance of courageous confrontation with the history of holocaustal horror. The absence of any reference to Yotam as husband and father seems to imply that the inability of the educator of the "new" Israelis to become a father to the Holocaust victim bears on the future generation of Israelis. The reception of the victim's 'didactic message' in Hareven's stories seems to indicate that in terms of Israel's continuation, some of the grief must be assuaged in order for the will to live to go on. Such attenuation, however, signifies a searing process of coming to terms with an irreparable loss.

Notes

1. S. Friedländer, "On the Representations of the Shoah in Present-Day Western Culture," in *Remembering for the Future: The Impact of the Holocaust on the Contemporary World* (Oxford: Pergamon Press, 1988), p. 3098.

2. For further accounts of Holocaust thematic in contemporary Israeli literature, see Alan Mintz, "Survivor and Bystanders," in *Hurban: Responses to Catastrophe in Hebrew Literature* (New York: Columbia University Press, 1984), pp. 239ff., and Gershon Shaked, "Afterword," in *Facing the Holocaust: Selected Israeli Fiction,* ed. Gila Ramras-Rauch and Joseph Michman-Melkman (Philadelphia: Jewish Publication Society, 1985), pp. 273–89.

3. S. Rimmon-Kenan, *Narrative Fiction: Contemporary Poetics* (London: Methuen, 1983), p. 100.

4. L. L. Melbourne, *Double Heart: Explicit and Implicit Texts in Bellow, Camus and Kafka* (New York: Peter Lang, 1986).

5. Ibid., pp. 20–21.

6. Ibid., p. 17.

7. W. Earle, *The Autobiographical Consciousness* (Chicago: Quadrangle Books, 1972), p. 144.

8. S. Hareven, "Ha-Ed" (The witness), in *L'Orech HaShurot* (Tel Aviv: Ramot, 1985), p. 52.

9. Ibid., pp. 52–53. All translations are mine—R. F. B.

10. Ibid., p. 52.

11. Ibid., p. 37.

12. Ibid., p. 41.

13. D. A. Foster, *Confession and Complicity in Narrative* (Cambridge: Cambridge University Press, 1987), p. 16.

14. Hareven, "Ha-Ed," p. 52.

15. Ibid., pp. 47–48.

16. I am referring to Irving Howe's description of himself and his fellow New York Jewish intellectuals who, in the thirties, "meant to declare themselves citizens of the world." After the Holocaust, however, this self-perception changed: "We might scorn our origins; we might crush America with discoveries of ardor; we might change our names. But we knew that but for an accident of geography we might also be now bars of soap." *The Decline of the New* (New York: Harcourt, Brace & World, 1970), p. 216.

17. A *sabra* is a prickly pear, a cactus; the term has come to designate an Israeli-born individual who, metaphorically, has a prickly exterior and a tender heart.

18. S. Hareven, "Twilight," trans. Miriam Arad, in *Facing the Holocaust: Selected Israeli Fiction,* ed. Gila Ramras-Rauch and Joseph Michman-Melkman (Philadelphia: Jewish Publication Society, 1985), p. 165.

19. Ibid., p. 167.

20. Ibid., p. 168.

21. S. Ezrahi, "Dan Pagis: The Holocaust and the Poetics of Incoherence," *Remembering the Future: The Impact of the Holocaust on the Contemporary World* (Oxford: Pergamon Press, 1988), pp. 2415–16.

22. Ibid., p. 2415.

23. "Twilight," p. 163.

24. J. Young, *Writing and Rewriting the Holocaust: Narrative and the Consequences of Interpretation* (Bloomington: Indiana University Press, 1988), p. 95.

25. "Twilight," p. 169.

26. Ibid., p. 167.

The Influence of the Holocaust on My Work

SAVYON LIEBRECHT

In the last few years Israel has experienced an outburst of creativity in all fields of art on the subject of the Holocaust. Most of the creators are children of Holocaust survivors, so that I believe I speak for many others. In this respect, when I say "I," it is a collective "I" rather than a personal one.

The influence of the Holocaust on my work cannot be separated from the influence of the Holocaust on my life. The very subjects which trouble you and inspire you and haunt you as a person, are those which are—in all sorts of disguises—going to reveal themselves in your work. And since the Holocaust is the event which, more than any other, has left its marks on my life, it has become a subject in my work.

I feel that I must provide some details about myself to make my points clear: Both my parents are Holocaust survivors. Born in Poland, each of them was the only survivor of a large family. My father was married and the father of a baby when the war broke out; and he lost them, too. After the war, my parents met and married in Germany, where I was born. I was a baby when we came to live in Israel.

One more thing is important to state: I know almost nothing about their past. They kept total silence in our home about their Holocaust experiences. To this day, I don't know how many brothers and sisters my parents had. I don't know their names, I don't know what happened to them during the war, and I don't know in which concentration camps my father was held. But I do know that he went through several.

People who observe the dynamics of behavior in homes of Holocaust survivors are able to make a very clear distinction between two kinds of homes. In one, there is obsessive talk about the Holocaust, and any subject that comes up—from a shoelace to a piece

125

of bread—leads directly to memories from the ghetto and the concentration camps. The other kind of home reacts by keeping a total silence. My guess is that most creative people in the arts grew up in homes of the second sort, because there is nothing like silence to trigger creativity. Every child needs explanations about the world around him, but a child who grows up in such a home feels that questions are undesirable. So he starts supplying his own answers, and begins to exercise his imagination from a very early age.

The silence in the homes of Holocaust survivors is unique. It is a silence that covers pain and dark secrets, and it takes time until the child who grows up in such a home understands that this secret is not a personal one but a national, or even a universal, one. Until he understands that—and it happens when he is about eight or ten—he grows up believing that there is something terribly wrong with him and his family. Homes of Holocaust survivors are quiet homes: parents don't speak about the past; they don't speak about their thoughts; they don't speak about their feelings. In a way, the children in such homes are compelled to develop alternative ways of expression.

If you see art as a form of communication, the silence in their homes is the key to the children becoming, one day, artists. I remember myself creating dozens of biographies for myself, because I had an endless open space to be anyone: an Indian princess, an African slave, a tightrope walker, and an Eskimo. You had no definite identity—you had no history and no ancestors—so you could become anyone you chose. When I write a story today and have to enter into a character's mind and observe the world through his eyes, it comes naturally to me. I spent years in my childhood doing exactly this.

There is one more thing to add about how this silence influenced my work. As communication in such a home is not exercised verbally, you learn to understand things that are not spoken aloud; you exercise a sort of mind reading. As a child you reach out with all your senses to try and figure out what is going on around you. You learn to understand the real meaning of sentences that have a double meaning, and there comes a time when words do not mislead you. This skill becomes useful when, one day, you find that very often you don't need words to understand things; you can look at two people sitting together and know what is going on between them. In other words, your life has made you an experienced observer. You have acquired an insight into situations and moods. I believe that, as a writer, this is my main skill.

I'd like now to turn to two of my stories, "Cutting" and "Hayuta's Engagement Party." First I will tell their content briefly.

Some years ago there was a plague of lice in Israel, especially in kindergartens. The children would be sent home with little notes pinned to their clothes, telling the mothers that lice were found on the children's heads and that they should take care of it. My story "Cutting" takes place on such a day, which also happens to be a little girl's birthday. She is four years old and her parents are busy arranging the birthday party. Her grandmother, who is a Holocaust survivor, comes to fetch her home and reads that note about the lice. The moment she understands what it is about, she gets frantic. It brings back all the memories of the concentration camp, and she starts cutting the girl's hair—her beloved granddaughter's hair—in the most brutal way.

"Hayuta's Engagement Party" tells about an old man, an eighty-year-old Holocaust survivor, who has long kept silent about what happened to him during the war. Forty years after the war, he gets into the habit of telling the most terrible stories at the table when the family meets—usually on Rosh Hashanah or on the Seder night. Apart from his daughter-in-law, who rebels against his stories, his family listens to them quietly. But when his granddaughter—again his beloved granddaughter—has her engagement party, she makes him promise not to talk about his memories of the Holocaust in front of the new in-laws. As a result of his conflict—unable to talk because of the promise which he tries to keep, and unable *not* to talk because it has become a mechanism stronger than himself— the grandfather dies in the middle of the party.

These two stories were chosen by chance, because they happen to be translated into English. But when I sat down to write this article, I was amazed to make some discoveries about the similarity between them. I could see that they both deal with the same basic situation, and that they are really the same story in different guises.

The first obvious similarity touches on the background; two celebrations—a birthday party and an engagement party. I find this interesting and not at all accidental, because during the week, people are busy with daily activities. It is only during festive family celebrations that the memories float to the surface. It is only then, when families get together, that the Holocaust survivor has the losses visualized and can see how few members of the family are left. Only then can he compare the current family meetings with the ones he remembers from the time before the war, with the large families and all the grandparents, uncles, aunts, and cousins.

The other common point is the rebellious figure. In both stories some very hard words are spoken out against the main characters. In "Cutting" the little girl's mother shouts at her husband: "Your mother is just not normal. I told you a long time ago. She has got some screws loose from that Holocaust. I won't let her near my child again." In "Hayuta's Engagement Party" Shifra says: "We have heard enough. Don't we have Memorial Day and Holocaust Day and what have you? They never let you forget for a minute. So why do I need to be reminded of it at every meal? The moment he opens his mouth—the holiday is over."

Both rebellious women are daughters-in-law. I wasn't aware of this when writing the stories; it struck me only recently when preparing this article. But it seems such a correct choice, because only an in-law could have said these things. No child of a Holocaust survivor could have uttered such words. It had to be put in the mouth of an outsider—an outsider who became part of the family and is now involved enough to have the right to say these things. And, in a way, the voice of a daughter-in-law is a subconscious device to express my own feelings. For being a child of a Holocaust survivor is a heavy burden. Indeed, in some fashion, being a child of a Holocaust survivor is more difficult than being a Holocaust survivor himself.

Let me try to explain: I am not referring to physical pain or suffering, because what Holocaust survivors went through is beyond imagination. However, if you believe—and many psychologists do—that childhood is the most influential part of one's life in determining the emotional stability of the person one is about to become, and if you consider statistics which say that most Holocaust survivors were over the age of fifteen when the war broke out, then you must agree that my parents were given better chances than I to become stable people. They each had a normal childhood and they coped with the horrors of the Holocaust as adults.

Whereas I was born into the Holocaust to parents who were broken, who had lost everything—including their language, their cultural background, and their optimism. In puberty, when it is time for a growing person to follow one's natural instincts and rebel against parents, you find that you are unable to do so, because you have grown up knowing that you mustn't inflict pain on them. So that, maybe, the daughters-in-law are, in a very hidden, unconscious way, a literary device to let out aggression, an expression of a late rebellion.

There is no doubt that the little girl in each of the two stories is very precious to her grandparents. And yet both stories end in disaster. What does this mean in terms of the writing hand? I think that perhaps on a symbolic level, people who have gone through a trauma have it so deeply imprinted in their behavior that they unconsciously repeat a familiar compulsive pattern. On a more practical level, I think it conveys some sort of distrust of Holocaust survivors, because you have learned that they are not reliable. They love you very dearly, and you are the center of the world for them—but they are too weak for you to rely on. Their children—in these stories their grandchildren—learn that there is a wide gap between intentions and deeds. But it could also mean that when it comes to explaining about the Holocaust, new ways of measuring things have to be invented, because the criteria with which we judge events under normal circumstances stop being valid when we refer to Holocaust survivors. Even after forty years, they are overpowered by the codes of behavior which they adopted then, and in certain moments the reality of the concentration camp overcomes current reality. In these moments, cutting off the lice-ridden hair, or telling stories of the camps at the table, seems natural. This is the core of the drama and the tragedy in these two stories.

The most obvious similarity between the two stories is that they both deal with a grandparents-grandchildren relationship. This is a topic which interests me in many other stories, some of which do not touch upon the Holocaust at all. This may be surprising, because I belong to a generation that grew up with no grandparents. And so all my stories about grandparents are based on an imaginary biography. On the other hand, it is a most understandable act to try and compensate yourself for what reality has deprived you of. And so, in my stories, I keep creating grandparents for myself, as well as the uncles and aunts and cousins I never had. But mostly I create grandparents.

I believe a child needs grandparents for normal development. In a mythical sense, it is the grandfather who tells stories. Going back to my earlier theory about silence, I know that since I belong to a generation that had no grandfathers to tell us stories, and since our parents kept such a total silence, I had to tell stories to myself. Mostly because the best way to break a silence is by telling stories.

Contributors

AVRAHAM BALABAN, Department of African and Asian Languages and Literatures, University of Florida

LIVIA BITTON-JACKSON, Hebraic and Judaic Division, Department of Classics, Lehman College, The City University of New York

RACHEL FELDHAY BRENNER, Department of Hebrew and Semitic Studies, University of Wisconsin—Madison

WILLIAM D. BRIERLEY, doctoral candidate, New College, Oxford

ZILLA JANE GOODMAN, Department of Near Eastern Judaic and Hellenic Languages and Literatures, Ohio State University

SAVYON LIEBRECHT, Israeli writer

ABRAHAM MARTHAN, Department of Hebrew Language and Literature, Gratz College

LEON I. YUDKIN, Department of Near East Studies, University of Manchester